Praise for *I Love*

This book took my breath away. It puts the dream within reach. It decodes the seemingly uncrackable mysteries of marriage and translates them into understandable, accessible, and manageable steps. Buy this book—and the workbooks—for everyone within your circle. Good marriages are contagious. Spread the wealth.

Diane Sollee, Founder and Director of Coalition for Marriage, Family, and Couples Education

I love Les and Leslie Parrott! They're not only experts—they're normal. They even fight with each other once in a while! You'll love this insightful, practical book. It should be required reading for every couple.

Dr. Kevin Leman, Author of *Sex Begins in the Kitchen*

As a therapist who has devoted her career to helping couples make their marriages more loving, and a woman married to the same man for over two decades, I think I know a thing or two about what it takes to make relationships work. But now, after reading this wonderful book, I know more.

It should be required reading for every engaged, newlywed, and veteran couple! I love it!

Michele Weiner-Davis, Author of *Divorce Busting*

In *I Love You More*, Les and Leslie Parrott have given us a book that is blatantly honest about the roadblocks to a meaningful marriage, and extremely practical about how to make the most of the detour routes while getting back on the main highway. For those who do not want to get lost in the wilderness, this book provides an excellent road map to a successful marriage.

Gary D. Chapman, Ph.D., Author of *The Five Love Languages*

No one can escape bad moments in marriage, but no one is meant to drown in the difficulty. Les and Leslie Parrott provide the wisdom to help every marriage make a safe and satisfying course through turbulent waters. They speak with honesty, humor, and grace. Their message is grounded in solid research, counseling experience, and their own bumps and bruises from life. This book is not only compelling, it is an essential guide for all of us who seek the best for our marriage when it bumps into bad things.

Dan B. Allender, Ph.D., Author of *Intimate Allies*

No married couple can fail to benefit from the wisdom and sound advice found in this book.

David Popenoe, Professor of Sociology, Codirector, The National Marriage Project, Rutgers University

Les and Leslie Parrott have written a deeply compassionate book to guide all of us along the marriage path. Whether your relationship has run into a few speed bumps or some daunting mountains, the Parrotts' wisdom will see you through.

Scott M. Stanley, Ph.D., University of Denver, Coauthor of *A Lasting Promise*

Les and Leslie Parrott have a message every married couple needs to hear. *I Love You More* is the best toolbox I've seen for helping couples survive and thrive in the midst of life's inevitable difficulties. Whether it's busyness or boredom, infidelity or infertility, Les and Leslie provide solid solutions that are guaranteed to strengthen your marriage.

Gary Smalley, Author of *Bound by Honor*

Every marriage, sooner or later, goes through tough times. Guaranteed. We only wish we would have had the wisdom Les and Leslie offer in this book before we entered our own valley of suffering. You can be sure we'll use it with other couples—and it will be required reading for our adult children before they get married.

Dave and Jan Dravecky

Formerly Titled *When Bad Things Happen to Good Marriages*

i love you more

How Everyday Problems
Can Strengthen Your Marriage

Drs. Les & Leslie Parrott

GRAND RAPIDS, MICHIGAN 49530 USA

We want to hear from you. Please send your comments about this book to us in care of zreview@zondervan.com. Thank you.

ZONDERVAN™

I Love You More
Copyright © 2001, 2005 by Les and Leslie Parrott
Formerly titled *When Bad Things Happen to Good Marriages*

Requests for information should be addressed to:
Zondervan, *Grand Rapids, Michigan 49530*

Library of Congress Cataloging-in-Publication Data

Parrott, Les.
    I love you more : how everyday problems can strengthen your marriage /
Les and Leslie Parrott.
      p. cm.
    Rev. ed. of: When bad things happen to good marriages. c2001.
      Includes bibliographical references.
    ISBN-10: 0-310-25738-7
    ISBN-13: 978-0-310-25738-7
    1. Spouses—Religious life. 2. Marriage—Religious aspects—Christianity.
I. Parrott, Leslie L., 1964– II. Parrott, Les. When bad things happen to good
marriages. III. Title.
    BV4596.M3P38   2005
    248.8'44—dc22   2005004288

Published in association with Yates & Yates, LLP, Attorneys and Counselors, Suite 1000, Literary Agent, Orange, CA.

Interior design by Beth Shagene

Printed in the United States of America

05 06 07 08 09 10 11 12 /❖ DCI/ 10 9 8 7 6 5 4 3 2 1

To Greg and Connie Smith,
a couple who has weathered more
than their fair share of bad things
and whose marriage is doubly strong
because of it

contents

real-life problem solvers

Below is a listing of some true stories you will find throughout this book. Each story focuses on a specific marital struggle and is written by a courageous couple who strengthened their marriage in spite of their struggle. We offer these contributions as a source of inspiration and examples of practical problem solving.

workbook exercises

Below is a listing of the exercises and self-tests you will find in the two workbooks we have designed to go along with this book (one for husbands and one for wives). In each chapter we will point you to a specific exercise to work on once you have read a particular section. This list can serve as a quick reference to the location of the exercises within this book.

acknowledgments

Some authors, when talking of their works, say, my book, my commentary, and my history," said Pascal. "I recommend them to say, our book, because in general they contain much more of what belongs to other people than to themselves." How right he is. The book you hold in your hands is testament to that fact.

As always, we could have never completed this project without the help of so many supportive people—starting with our friends at Zondervan. From Bruce Ryskamp and Scott Bolinder, to Sandy Vander Zicht, Lori VandenBosch, and Angela Scheff, to John Topliff and Greg Stielstra and Jessica Westra, to Joyce Ondersma and Jackie Aldridge, to Stan Gundry and everyone else on the Z team who has invested so much of themselves in our shared vision—we could never convey the depth of gratitude we feel toward all of you. We are privileged to know you not only as consummate professionals, but as friends whose company we thoroughly enjoy.

We sent an early draft of this book to a variety of readers and invited them to mark up the manuscript and make suggestions. This feedback proved invaluable. So we are especially grateful to Jim and Nancy Smith, Jeff and Stacy Kemp, Tim and Kerry Dearborn, Greg and Connie Smith, and Scott and Debbie Daniels. Each of you provided information that bolstered the content of this book, and it is a far better project because of your honest input.

We are also deeply grateful to the fifteen couples who allowed us to look into their good marriages and learn how they coped with a bad thing. These are couples who had the courage to show us how they dealt with struggles we had no right to ask about—and yet they willingly opened their hearts and homes to let us learn of their real-life solutions to tough marital problems. These couples are all listed, along with their various topics, on a previous page.

Jon Anderson lent us his research abilities for this project. His library prowess and skill became invaluable as we combed though mountains of marriage research for this book.

Janice Lundquist goes beyond the call of duty on a regular basis. Her dedication and support of our efforts is matched only by the friendship we share with her. We are eternally grateful, not only for the ways you help us manage our professional lives, but for the ways you enrich our personal lives as well.

Our students and fellow faculty and staff, as well as the administration at Seattle Pacific University, have provided a safe harbor for our work. Over the years, you have allowed our Center for Relationship Development to sink its roots into our campus and grow in ways that were not always predictable or traditional. That's not easy for an academic institution, and we are appreciative.

During the final stages of our work on this project we were invited by the Governor and First Lady of Oklahoma, Frank and Kathy Keating, to become their "marriage ambassadors" and work with them on their statewide marriage initiative. It has been a true honor to link arms with Jerry Regier, Howard Hendricks, Mary Myrick, JoAnn Eason, and their capable staff, Kendy, Jessica, and Josh, as well as colleagues at Oklahoma State University, and so many others who are working to help good marriages battle bad things across the Sooner State.

Finally, we want to express our appreciation to the thousands of couples who have participated in our Soul Mates Seminars around the country over the last few years. Your stories, your questions, and your desire to pursue lifelong love became the catalyst for this book. You are an inspiration. We hope you and couples like you will find in this book new tools for making your marriage everything it was meant to be.

Les and Leslie Parrott
Seattle, Washington

You can tell a good, surviving marriage by the expression
in the partners' eyes — like those of sailors who have shared
the battles against foul weather.

Pam Brown

more today than yesterday

For you see, each day I love you more
Today more than yesterday and less than tomorrow.
Rosemonde Gerard

No marriage—no matter how good—is immune to everyday problems. Some problems quietly sneak up on us without a whisper. Others are about as subtle as a military band.

However they arrive, problems come part and parcel with married life. Each and every couple suffers private problems and sometimes public pitfalls. Sexual unfulfillment that quietly hardens our hearts. Financial debt that shrouds us in shame. Hope deferred by the anguish of infertility. Communication meltdowns that tempt us to quit trying. Addictions that drive us into secret lives. Problems with anger that cause loved ones to walk on egg shells. Personal pain from an abusive past that keeps us from loving in the present. The list could go on and on. The everyday problems, both big and small, that interfere with a good marriage are countless.

We all know that even the best marriages have problems. What you may not know is that your problems can become the tipping point for a deeper love between you. Truth be told, everyday problems are what compel a couple to say, "I love you more today than yesterday."

So we dedicate this book to every couple who started out smoothly on the path of love and eventually stubbed their toe on something they didn't expect. And that's all of us. This is a book for *every* couple. For who among us can claim to have been so lucky in love that nothing has ever jolted our relationship? Who among us is so skilled, so adept at love, that we have kept every bad thing from interfering?

Like we said, we all know problems happen to good marriages. That's not the point we're making with this book. And we're not here to tell you that marriage is hard work. You already know that, too. We're also not here to say that with some effort you can protect your marriage from problems in the future. That's a lie. Instead, we want to show you how the inevitable problems in life that come between two loving people don't have to harm their marriage. We intend to show you how the very opposite, in fact, can be true: that problems are to a marriage what cold water is to burning metal; it strengthens, tempers, intensifies, but does not destroy it.

I've fallen in love many times . . .
always with you.
Author unknown

In practical terms, we will give you the five most important tools your marriage needs to successfully battle everyday problems. Among other things, we'll show you the one thing you can change right now to make your marriage better. We've put together two no-nonsense workbooks—one for the husband and one for the wife—filled with exercises designed to help the two of you pull together when life tries to pull you apart. As you are reading along in each chapter of the book, we will point you toward a specific set of exercises in the workbooks. This method creates a kind of self-paced path toward internalizing and applying the book's message.

The bottom line of this book is simple: We are here to show you that your marriage is not as good as it's going to get. For once you learn the secrets of how everyday problems can bring you closer together, you will love each other more. More than you did yesterday ... and less than tomorrow.

———

You have to walk carefully in the beginning of love;
the running across fields into your lover's arms
can only come later
when you're sure they won't laugh if you trip.
Jonathan Carroll

———

love is not enough

A marriage survives and thrives when a couple learns
to use problems to their advantage.

All beginnings are lovely.
French proverb

Two days after our wedding in Chicago, Les and I were nestled into a cottage, surrounded by towering timbers along the picturesque Oregon coast. A few miles to the south of us were the famous coastal sand dunes where we planned to ride horses later that week. And up the coast was a quaint harbor village where we thought we might spend another day leisurely looking at shops and eating our dinner by candlelight in a rustic inn some friends recommended. Other than that, we had nothing on our itinerary for the next five days except enjoying the beach and each other, rain or shine.

Neither of us could have dreamed up a scenario that would have been better for our honeymoon. Not that everything was perfect. For starters, we accidentally locked ourselves out of our rental car the day after we arrived. I was commenting on how the sun was trying to poke its way out of some clouds when Les realized the keys were in the ignition and all the doors were locked.

"You stay here in the cabin," Les said, taking his first stab at being an everything's-under-control kind of husband. "I'm going to walk to that filling station on the main road and get some help."

"I'll go with you," I responded.

"Are you sure? It might rain."

"It'll be fun; let's go."

We walked and talked the two or three miles to find a pay phone, where we made arrangements for the locksmith to pick us up and take us back to our car. Sitting on a curb, we waited, saying nothing. Les was fiddling with a stick he'd picked up on our walk when I realized several minutes had passed and neither of us had said a word. It was an easy stillness, though; a kind of eloquent voicelessness where we were content, comfortable, to not talk.

I think it was there and then, quietly sitting on a curb next to a phone booth under a cloudy sky, that the thought hit me like a ray of light. I had captured true love. The thing I'd been chasing ever since I was old enough to know it could be sought was now in my possession. I had married a man who loved me deeply, just as I loved him. We committed ourselves to love together, forever. Love's ethereal mysteries were now unfolding before my very eyes. Its elusive qualities were fading. True love was no longer out of reach. The very opposite, in fact, was true. While I stood by doing nothing, love was enveloping my being. I'm not talking about the dizzying effects of falling in love that happen in the early starry-eyed stages of a new relationship. Les and I had dated for nearly seven years before we found ourselves married and honeymooning on the Oregon coast.

> Whoso loves believes the impossible.
> *Elizabeth Barrett Browning*

The love I'm talking about experiencing that day was clear-eyed and grounded. There was no sunset on the horizon, no piped-in background music. This was reality and I was simply taking it in, relishing the silence and stillness of having no other purpose than that of being together. Husband and wife. We had created a marriage. And it was good. So good was this love we had at the beginning that we could practically live on it. And we did, for a time.

Can We Keep a Good Thing Going?

Like most couples deeply in love, Les and I longed to find ways to make our love endure even before we were married. Part of the impetus for our vision came from reading *A Severe Mercy*, the real-life love story about Sheldon and Davy Vanauken, two lovers who not only dreamed about building a soulful union, but devised a concrete strategy for doing so that they called their "Shining Barrier." Its goal: to make their love invulnerable. Its plan: to share *everything*. Everything! If one of them liked something, they decided, there must be something to like in it—and the other must find it. Whether it be poetry, strawberries, or an interest in ships, Sheldon and Davy committed to share every single thing either of them liked. That way they would create a thousand strands, great and small, that would link them together. They reasoned that by sharing everything they would become so close that it would be impossible, unthinkable, for either of them to suppose that they could ever recreate such closeness with anyone else. Total sharing, they felt, was the ultimate secret of a love that would last forever.[1]

To be the watch upon the walls of the Shining Barrier, Sheldon and Davy established what they called the Navigators' Council. It was an inquiry into the state of their union. More than once a month they would intentionally talk about their relationship and evaluate their activities by asking, Is this best for our love?

> There is no more lovely, friendly, and charming relationship, communion, or company than a good marriage.
>
> *Martin Luther*

It's a great question. Why not raise the Shining Barrier as Sheldon and Davy did? Why not create a shield to protect one's love? After all, who hasn't seen the soul of a marriage perish because the couple took love for granted? Ceasing to do things together, finding separate interests, many couples turn their "we" into "I" as their love becomes lifeless. Even before we were married we observed a subtle separateness creeping into some marriages with barely a notice—each of them going off to their separate jobs in separate worlds, while their apartness was quietly tearing at their union. Why let this happen to us? Why not raise the Shining Barrier?

Something about guarding against losing the glory of love struck a chord with us—just as it does with every couple on the brink of marriage. But is it possible? Is it within the realm of human capability to keep love always protected from harm? And even if it were, is love enough to sustain a marriage? The answer, in our opinion, is no. And the Vanauken story proves it. Sheldon and Davy did everything possible to preserve their love, but in the end, they couldn't. Death stole their togetherness as Davy lay dying in a hospital bed.

We'll say it again. Love cannot protect a marriage from harm, and love, by itself, is not enough to sustain even the most loving couples.

Exercise 1: Taking Inventory of Your Marriage

Before progressing further into this chapter, we urge you to take inventory of the good and the bad in your relationship. This initial exercise will set the stage for the work you do in chapters to come. The exercise is found in the accompanying *I Love You More Workbooks* (note that there is one workbook for husbands and another one for wives). The exercise will help you and your partner identify what is currently making your love life tougher than it needs to be and what is already helping you make it better.

Love Is Not Enough to Make a Marriage Good

It's a rare week when our postman in Seattle does not deliver a wedding invitation to our door. Because we work with so many engaged couples through our teaching, seminars, and counseling, we get invited to more weddings than we can ever attend. And the ones we do attend always remind us how glorious the beginning of lifelong love is. We stand up with this individual and make a declaration in front of friends and family concerning the convincing nature of our love and how it will endure a lifetime. We vow right then and there to dedicate the rest of our lives to the pursuit, discovery, testing, enjoying, and continual renewal of this love. We are so convinced of the enduring quality of this good love that we stake our very lives on it. We vow to love "until death do us part."

Without love there would be no wedding, and certainly no marriage. Love is the catalyst for commitment. Love is what insures that every marriage starts out good. But sooner or later every good marriage bumps into negative things. And that's when honest couples discover that love, no matter how good, is never enough.

Let's make this clear: We all entered marriage confident our union would not simply survive but thrive. Our confidence was built and bolstered by our love. But here's the kicker: One cannot completely guard one's love against the things that diminish it (not even Sheldon and Davy could do that). What's more, love in itself is seldom sturdy enough to support a couple when they inevitably run into bad things. In fact, the loss of love is given as a major reason

> For one human being to love another: that is perhaps the most difficult of all our tasks, the ultimate, the last test and proof, the work for which all other work is but preparation.
>
> *Rainer Marie Rilke*

for marital dissolution.[2] Love, while being a good catalyst for marriage, cannot sustain it alone.

We have counseled countless couples who cling to the sentimental romantic notion of love expressed in songs, movies, and novels. It is a notion that leads most of us into a destructive marital myth that says, *Everything good in this relationship should get better in time.* But the truth is, not everything gets better. Many things improve because of marriage, but some things become more difficult. Every successful marriage, for example, requires necessary losses. For starters, marriage means coming to terms with new limits on one's independence. It means giving up a carefree lifestyle. Even to people who have dreamed for years about getting married and who think of themselves as hating to be alone, marriage still cannot help but come as an invasion of privacy and independence. No one has ever been married without being surprised at the sheer intensity of this invasion. And so, for many, they run into their first real challenge to love. But it will not be their last.

> What greater thing is there for two human souls than to feel that they are joined for life—to strengthen each other in all labor, to rest on each other in all sorrow, to minister to each other in all pain.
>
> *George Eliot*

Like two weary soldiers taking cover in a bunker, every couple is bewildered by constant assaults to their love life. Marriage is continually bombarded by unpredictable instances that interfere with being the kind of lovers we want to be. We are torn apart by busy schedules, by words we wish we could take back, and in short, by not giving all that love demands.

"Love asks for everything," writes Mike Mason. "Not just for a little bit, or a whole lot, but for everything."[3] And how hard it is to give everything! Indeed, it is impossible. We can establish a Shining Barrier or make a symbolic gesture of giving all, even declare it quite dramatically at a wedding ceremony, but that is just a start, a mere message of intention. It is only when we move beyond the "moon of honey," as the French put it, that our love is truly tested. And no one, no matter how loving, can stand up to the test of not only giving everything one *owns* but everything one *is*. Be certain of this: You and your spouse will fail at love. Why? Because no mere mortal can ever live by romantic love alone.

Husbands and wives get hurt in love. Bad things happen. Nevertheless, for the couple who is able to accept that not everything good gets better in marriage and who matures together in love, there is a great surprise in store: their marriage, though bandied about by a myriad of bad things, can remain good, or at the very least get good once more.

What Makes a Marriage Good?

Ask most people this question and you'll undoubtedly hear something about love. But ask those who have given it serious thought, who have dedicated themselves to study and research of the topic, and you'll hear a different answer. Better yet, ask this question of couples who have a good marriage in spite of everything they've encountered, and you'll hear the answer that matters most. That's what we did, and it became the reason for writing this book. Here's what they told us: *A good marriage is built by two people's capacity to adjust to negative things*. In survey after survey, when we asked couples to crystallize their thoughts on what makes a marriage successful, that was their answer. And when we pushed them to flesh out that answer, we learned the secrets these smart couples hold.

> Passion, though a bad regulator,
> is a powerful spring.
> *Ralph Waldo Emerson*

A good marriage is made up of . . . two people who take
ownership for the good as well as the bad. They are
a responsible couple.

A good marriage is made up of . . . two people believing
good wins over bad. They are a hopeful couple.

A good marriage is made up of . . . two people walking
in each other's shoes. They are an empathic couple.

A good marriage is made up of . . . two people healing the
hurts they don't deserve. They are a forgiving couple.

A good marriage is made up of . . . two people living the
love they promise. They are a committed couple.

Exercise 2: Exploring Your Marital Armament

If you are like most couples, it may help to measure where you and your partner
stand on each of these five traits of a good marriage. Are you more optimistic than
your partner, for example, while your partner is more forgiving than you are? This
exercise in your workbooks gives you an opportunity to assess each of these important qualities in yourselves.

From all that we can gather, these five qualities are the armament used to
protect good couples from destruction: ownership, hope, forgiveness, empathy,
and commitment. And it is these five qualities that we devote later parts of this
book to, giving you practical ways to cultivate them in your own marriage. Before
we get there, however, there is an important question that needs consideration.
It is one that lingers in the mind of every couple whose love has bumped into
negative things. And how you answer it will determine how well you learn to protect the love you cherish. *Why do problems occur in good marriages?* We explore
possible answers in the next chapter.

For Reflection

1. As you consider the beginning of your marriage, do you recall a time when you felt "enveloped" by love? How do you describe such an experience, and how likely is it in later passages of marriage?
2. Do you identify with Sheldon and Davy Vanauken in their pursuit to protect their love from harm with a "Shining Barrier"? What have you done, in concrete terms, to guard your love for each other?
3. What do you make of this idea that to survive bad things, a good marriage needs more than love? Do you agree? If so, why? If not, how do you support your position?
4. As you begin this study of good marriages bumping into bad things, what hopes and fears do you carry with you?

Take away love and our earth is a tomb.
Robert Browning

---

why every marriage has everyday problems

All your difficulties can be traced to one of five sources —
and knowing the source makes all the difference.

> There can be no deep disappointment
> where there is not deep love.
> *Martin Luther King Jr.*

Jack and Rose. Two simple names that are as synonymous with love as Romeo and Juliet. Perhaps more so. Writer and director James Cameron dreamed up their steamy love story for his impressive cinematic tale of the fateful voyage of the *Titanic*, which became the highest-grossing movie of all time. Despite the fact that the film opens with eerie footage of the real downed liner and closes with gruesome reconstructed scenes of passengers plummeting down the ship's decks while others are freezing to death in the icy Atlantic, viewers of the film hardly gave it an ounce of emotional attention. The disaster was peripheral to the real story on screen, the story of Jack and Rose.

Jack is the quintessential charming young man, played by Leonardo DiCaprio. Rose, the impetuous beauty, played by Kate Winslet, is faced with an impending marriage to a villainous character that is sure to make her future life miserable. When Rose gazes at Jack, fascination quickly turns into longing and their longing into love, the kind movies are made of. It's a love in which neither lover discovers, much less has to tolerate, anything seriously objectionable in the other. The kind of love that doesn't occur in real life.

In a superb irony, this most romantic of fantasies is played out against one of history's most famous calamities. In the midst of dire peril, not only because of their sinking ship but because a jilted lover is chasing them with a loaded gun, Jack and Rose still love. Perhaps that's one of the reasons people were so drawn to this story. Perhaps it was the main reason some paid to see it a second and third time, then bought the DVD collector's edition to watch at home. And perhaps it's the reason the cruise ship business boomed as never before shortly after *Titanic* was released in theaters. Because of Jack and Rose, couples everywhere began searching for love on the high seas— without a seeming concern for the fact that the ship they were on sank. These couples, like all of us, are looking for the kind of love that runs into bad things, dare we say even an iceberg, and survives.

But alas, even in a cinematic fairytale, their love does not survive. It's cut short by Jack's death. And just like the reminiscent Rose in old age whom we see at the end of the movie, we are left with a searching question: Why?

A Question Every Couple Needs to Ask

The question of why love was cut short for this fictional couple is actually quite clear to anyone who studies literature. Almost all enduring love stories end the same way. Of course, the tragic twosome of Romeo and Juliet is a classic. So are Lancelot and Guinevere. Rhett and Scarlett. And now add to this list Jack and Rose. Each snuffed out their powerful love while the heat of passion was turned up full blast. Why? Because it couldn't last. The heat of passion was never meant to. Can you imagine Romeo and Juliet as a married couple ... going off to work ... paying bills ... grocery shopping? How about Jack and Rose? It's almost incongruous; at least it takes a lot of the luster off their love story.

Far more difficult to answer is the question that matters most. *Why do some couples manage to enjoy lasting love, despite facing the same circumstances that defeat others?* Have you thought about this? It's apparent to most observers that some couples run headfirst into a crisis and come out the other side stronger than they started, while others face similar problems and end up barely holding it together. But why? Are they just lucky? Not according to the couples we surveyed. These couples never counted on luck to see them through anything.

So what's the difference? The answer begins to unfold when we take a closer look at the question. Why do problems interfere with something as good as love and marriage? It's a question we've asked ourselves countless times in recent years. Too many couples close to us have hit rock bottom. It's one thing for us as professionals to see it in a counseling office, but quite another when we see it in friends and family. Nonetheless, we've seen firsthand how a secret addiction to alcohol can shatter a couple's trust in each other. We've seen how a person's sheer self-centeredness can erode feelings that once glued them together. We've seen, on at least two occasions, how an exposed affair can explode a family to smithereens. And we've seen marriages that self-destruct for reasons that are not even discernible. Each time we are left with little more than the question *why?* How could something like this happen to them? And in times of quiet soul-searching, we ask the same question of ourselves.

> We have a picture of the perfect partner, but we marry an imperfect person. Then we have two options. Tear up the picture and accept the person, or tear up the person and accept the picture.
>
> *J. Grant Howard Jr.*

You see, the misfortunes of good people are not only a problem to the people who suffer. They are a problem to all who wonder if the same thing could happen to us. We watch in horror when a marriage breaks up, like gawkers at a traffic accident, because we want to find some sign, some justification for it happening to "them" and not "us." But after seeing too many couples suffer problems, the question still remains: Why? It is perhaps the most important question couples these days can ask, so we will pose it again: Why do marriages have problems?

Our research points to at least five possibilities:

1. Some idealistic couples hold onto unfulfilled expectations.
2. Some restless couples have not studied their unexamined selves.
3. Some contented couples have not tapped into their unskilled potential.
4. Some unwitting couples continue to make unhealthy choices.
5. Some unfortunate couples run into unpredictable circumstances.

Exercise 3: Why Every Marriage Has Everyday Problems

After reading through these possibilities, we want to help you make this list more personal. We want to help you explore these reasons as they apply to your marriage relationship. This workbook exercise will help you discover which one of the causes you tend to lean toward most naturally. The reason this is important to understand, by the way, is that the more you understand your "why," the better prepared you are to discover your "how."

The goal of this chapter is to help you identify the reasons your marriage might be vulnerable to everyday problems, to answer for yourself "why bad things might happen to us." Later, we'll get to how you can better cope with difficulty, but exploring the reasons for the difficulty in the first place is paramount to progress.

We begin with, perhaps, the most obvious reason some couples bump into bad things, especially couples who are somewhat idealistic.

Reason One: Unfulfilled Expectations

There is a fly in the ointment of every good marriage. It's the disease-carrying insect of unmet expectations, and it leads to serious if not debilitating disappointment. Consider what causes you to experience disappointment. Someone, namely your spouse, or something, namely your marriage, has failed to fulfill your expectations. You had it all set up in your mind: the way your partner would be romantic with you, the way he or she would celebrate your birthday or make decisions with you, the way you would have dinner together, the way you would spend your weekends, or any number of scenarios you had envisioned. But it never materialized. Your wish fell fast and hard against reality. Maybe you readjusted your expectations, or maybe they still linger even after all these years.

That's what happened to Kimberly and Will. They were five years into their marriage when Kimberly unknowingly continued to drive a wedge between them because she didn't realize she had married an illusion of her own making—a husband that would think, feel, and behave exactly as she expected.

It came to the surface one night over lasagna, a dish they used to prepare together in their dating days.

"Are you crying?" Will asked while tucking a paper napkin around the front of his shirt collar. Kimberly responded with silence and sniffles. "What happened?" Will gently probed. "Are you okay?"

> We have been poisoned by fairy tales.
>
> *Anaïs Nin*

With a deep intake of breath, as though readying herself to submerge into something, Kimberly avoided eye contact with Will and said, "You know what happened."

"No, I really don't—but I have a feeling it involves me." Will was restraining his sometimes sarcastic tongue. "What did I do?"

"It's what you didn't do."

Still baffled, Will sat in stunned silence.

"Don't you see what you're eating?" said Kimberly.

Half afraid he might say the wrong thing, Will looked at the table, paused, and asked, "Lasagna?"

"You still don't get it, do you?"

Will put his fork down and sat dumbfounded while Kimberly dabbed her eyes with a paper napkin. "Oh! You're upset because I didn't make the lasagna with you," Will said, as though he had just solved one of those brain-teasers you buy at a game store. "I'm sorry, Kim, it didn't even occur to me when I came home. I'm so wrapped up in this thing at work. Why didn't you just remind me?"

"That's the point," Kimberly said. "If I have to remind you, it ruins the whole thing. You came home, looked at the mail, and went straight to your computer."

Kimberly has held onto an expectation that Will and she will always cook lasagna together. But, this time, like some others, Will got distracted and Kimberly got hurt. Her expectation did not match her husband's. Was she justified in getting upset? Maybe. Will, knowing how important this was to her, could have shown Kimberly more courtesy. And maybe Kimberly could have remembered that Will had a pressing project at work. Maybe both of them are to blame, or maybe neither.

The point is that expectations, even the seemingly insignificant ones, lead to problems when they are continually unfulfilled yet continually held tight. Many of us erect mental images of almost every facet of our relationship, unrealistic, unfair, biased, or otherwise. And these phantom images then become our inner focus. They steer our emotions and have the potential to set us up for failure. Not because we are fundamentally mismatched, but because our unmatched expectations lead us

> Love stories are only fit
> for the solace of people
> in the insanity of puberty.
> *Aleister Crowley*

there. After all, we have staked everything on this person we marry. We have defined our very selves in terms of this choice. And we eventually learn this person is not what we expected, or at least what we wished.

If you could sit in our counseling office, even for a single day, and eavesdrop on the conversations we have with hurting couples, you'd never underestimate the destructive potential of unfulfilled expectations. You might hear the story, for example, of an anguished husband whose expectation of his wife to stay home with the children was not met. Or you might hear a devastated wife tell how she expected her husband to include her on major decisions and how angry she was when he took a job in another state before discussing it with her. You might hear a husband confess the disappointment he has in his married sex life because his expectations have never been met. Expectations, both big and small, both realistic and unreasonable, plague countless couples.

Let's make this clear. Some things dishearten us in our marriage when we expect our partner to think, feel, and behave the way we want them to—and we won't change these expectations even over time. When this occurs, each unrealistic expectation is like a link in a heavy chain that increasingly binds us to a disappointing marriage.

If this is a major reason for your marriage hitting some rough spots, be assured that we will provide solutions to this common causal factor later in the book (especially in chapter six). For now, we encourage you to take a moment to turn to the next exercise in your workbook.

Exercise 4: What Did You Expect?

Almost every marriage, no matter how mature, holds onto unmet expectations. This workbook exercise will help you unearth expectations you may not even be aware of having. It will help you pinpoint why you wind up frustrated again and again over marriage matters that may be big or small.

Real-Life Problem Solvers

How We Overcame Unfulfilled Expectations

Scott and Debbie Daniels
Married in 1990

We knew we had an "expectation problem" within the first few hours of our marriage. I (Debbie) expected our first morning to be filled with tender moments spooning in bed, cuddling a bit before we had room service deliver our breakfast. Instead, I awoke to the sound of a television infomercial and my new husband on the phone ordering not room service but an expensive set of baseball cards. I could not believe my eyes and ears. "What are you doing?" I asked. Scott mumbled something about his great find as I pulled the covers over my head and wondered if I was dreaming. I wasn't. For the first three years of our marriage, it seemed every day revealed a new expectation about our relationship that we didn't seem to share.

Scott's Experience

When we got married, I had no idea that Debbie's head was filled with so many romantic expectations. We never talked about them. I suppose she made a lot of assumptions, and so did I. In fact, when she was surprised to find me ordering baseball cards that first morning, I laughed it off. It wasn't a concern to me. I just happened to see a good deal on TV while I was waiting for her to wake up. I was deeply in love with Debbie, and I have been since our very first date. I just didn't expect to have to show it like we lived in some romantic movie. After all, that was fantasy, and this was real life. Of course, she didn't see it that way.

Debbie's Experience

I grew up in a single-parent family. I never saw a husband and wife really relate. So, to make up for my lack of marital models, I fantasized about what marriage would look like. I pictured my husband carrying me to bed each night, leaving me love notes on my dresser, sending me flowers, and writing me poetry. To be honest, I expected my husband to be my knight in shining armor. I pictured romantic dinners and dreamed of sweet nothings whispered in my ear. But once we were married, I quickly learned that Scott was far more interested in sports scores or playing golf than he was in being a knight. I wondered if I'd married the wrong guy. After all, it wasn't so long ago that I broke off an engagement with another guy and met Scott. Maybe I had married him on the rebound. It seemed like nothing he did matched my expectations of a loving husband. Not in the least.

How We Solved the Problem

We can almost point to the spot where our marriage took a major turn for the better. It was in our third year that we began to talk honestly and openly about our expectations. We didn't hold back. We reviewed our short marital history and recounted how and where our faulty expectations had got us. We both loved each other; that wasn't the issue. The problem, we agreed, was how each of us expected our love to be expressed. I told Scott about my ideals, and he confessed that his loving expressions are, as he puts it, more "practical." For the first time, I set aside my high standards and listened to Scott tell me how he genuinely shows his love. That led to a process of learning each other's love language. For example, I now know that when Scott calls to be sure I arrived somewhere safely or when he checks the car before I get behind the wheel, it's his way of saying he treasures me.

I (Scott) have learned to value physical affection. I now know what a thoughtful card can do for Debbie's spirit. And I've learned that roses are prized even more when we can't afford them. Bottom line? We no longer try to read each other's mind. In fact, we have made a game of rating on a scale of one to ten how accurate our mind-readings are.

We've come a long way. We still have the baseball cards Scott ordered from the shopping network the first day of our marriage. We laugh every time we look at them. Truth be told, we have never been more happily married than we are today.

A Word to Other Couples

Be open and honest about your expectations of each other. The more you talk them through, the less likely they are to cause you trouble.

Reason Two: Unexamined Selves

Few would dispute the enormous impact of Greek philosopher Plato, pupil of Socrates and teacher of Aristotle. In his various dialogues he touched on virtually every problem that has occupied subsequent philosophers; his teachings have been among the most influential in the history of Western civilization, and his works are counted among the world's finest literature. And if you were to ask anyone in the know to quote him, more often than not, you would hear a simple sentence that has become his trademark: "The unexamined life is not worth living."

Plato probably didn't have marriage in mind when he said these now-famous words so long ago, but they could not be more relevant to today's couples. In the daily blur of activity that surrounds most marriages, self-examination, the kind requiring serious soul-searching, is precious and rare. When was the last time you set aside a few moments for nothing more than contemplating who you are in your marriage?

For some couples, the omission of self-examination is the root cause of why their relationship bumps into problems. How can this be? Because the unexamined self leads to two major problems that mess up a good marriage.

The first is what we call the *Blind Self*. This is made up of all the things known by your spouse and not known by you. Have you ever been in a public setting, maybe at a party, and you get a smudge on your face or a piece of food on your upper lip? It happens to everyone. But not everyone will point out the problem. It's embarrassing to most people—but not your spouse. He or she will waste no time in telling you what you don't know about your appearance and how to correct it. And you'll be grateful. What you may not appreciate is when your spouse does the same thing for personal problems you'd rather not admit. "You're quick tempered," your spouse may say. Or, "You sometimes come off as insensitive." *What?! How dare you try to tell me about myself.* When your spouse hits a tender spot, you immediately put up your guard and measure your defenses. It's only natural. It goes against our grain to hear information about our dark side, the part of us we wish weren't true. But this very information is vital to the life of a good marriage.

> And what's romance? Usually,
> a nice little tale where you have
> everything As You Like It,
> where rain never wets your jacket
> and gnats never bite your nose
> and it's always daisy-time.
>
> D. H. Lawrence

It's taken a while for me to learn this lesson. Receiving feedback on my foibles is not my idea of a good time. Les, on the other hand, seems to thrive on it. More than once he has caught me off guard with a simple question: "What would make me a better husband?" The first time he asked this I thought he was joking, but he meant it. And through the years I've learned from his example, sometimes painfully so. But it is well worth it.

Let me give you a quick example. I consider myself a good listener. I've not only had advanced training in my graduate work on this skill, I am naturally predisposed to lend an ear to friends, family, and almost anyone. But some time ago, I discovered something about my listening style that irritated some people— including Les. "Are you aware of how often you finish my sentences," he said, "and how often you are wrong when you do?" *What?!* "I know you are well intentioned," he continued, "but I've seen you do this a lot and it's kind of annoying." Les gave me some examples of how I put words into another's mouth to let that person know I'm tracking, that I understand what he or she is saying. "I don't like it when you jump to conclusions about what I'm saying; it sometimes comes off like you are getting impatient with me." He was right. As tough as it was to hear, Les showed me a part of my Blind Self and helped me change my behavior, as well as my marriage, for the better.

Those who have ears to hear a timely critique from their partner reduce their blind spots. Those that don't, live a life of denial that is bound to interfere with a good marriage.

Exercise 5: The Big Question

Take a moment right now to ponder this important question: "What would make me a better spouse?" Our exercise in the workbooks will guide you in a thought-provoking experience of helping you take some of your blinders off to become the kind of partner you want to be. Every married couple can benefit from this.

The second major problem that results from a lack of soul-searching is found in what we call the *Hidden Self*. This is everything that is known by you and not your spouse. Each of us has a natural, built-in desire to be known, but we often stifle our vulnerability out of fear. We're afraid of being seen as too emotional or not emotional enough, as too assertive or not assertive enough. In short, we're afraid of rejection, even from the person who loves us the most. *If he knew the real me, he'd never love me*, we say to ourselves. The result? We hide parts of ourselves from our spouse to protect us against this potential rejection, whether it is real or imaginary.

You may be wondering what kind of hiding we're talking about. It's not so much about dishonesty as it is about being vulnerable. And it could have to do with anything, big or small. Maybe you don't confess that you lost fifty dollars while at the grocery store for fear you'll look foolish to your mate. You don't tell your partner that you have serious doubts about God for fear he or she won't understand. You keep a dark secret about being sexually abused as a child for fear that your spouse will view you as dirty. And the longer you keep your secrets, the more locked up you become, until you are even hiding parts of yourself from you. That's when you wonder why your good marriage has turned so bad. It's because your Hidden Self is keeping you from receiving the love you long for.

> If love . . . means that one person absorbs the other, then no real relationship exists any more. Love evaporates; there is nothing left to love. The integrity of self is gone.
>
> *Annie Oakley*

We know a couple, deeply in love, who had been married more than a dozen years when she dropped a bombshell. It was a few days after a trip they took through the town where she grew up as a girl that her husband found her sitting at the kitchen table in tears. It was late at night. "What's wrong?" he asked. He knelt down near her chair, and she asked him to sit across the table from her.

"I want to tell you something you don't know about me," she said. Her husband's heart began to race as she sobbed without speaking. He gave her time, and once she was composed she laid out a story of horrific sexual abuse that she endured as a child. In their twelve years of marriage, he sometimes suspected something like this (especially when watching certain movies and so on), but he had never heard a word about it until that night. Her secret was locked away in her Hidden Self.

The Blind Self can drive us to denial. The Hidden Self can move us to suspicion. Both distort reality. No wonder the unexamined self causes some good marriages to bump into bad problems. (We'll learn more about how to cope with and change the unexamined self in later chapters—especially chapter three.)

Reason Three: Unskilled Couples

Every marriage has a deficiency. It may be money management, sexual tension, problems with in-laws, unbalanced workloads, conflict resolution, difficulties with communication, anger, dishonesty, or anything else. This deficiency or weakness is a bad thing that spoils good things about the relationship.[1] If it weren't for this one thing, a couple might see everything else in a more positive light. It is the proverbial one bad apple that spoils the whole bunch.

Every summer, usually in July, for the last several years we have met with a number of other marriage specialists from around the country, people who have given their careers to understanding what makes marriage work and what doesn't. We sit around conference tables, talk over lunch, meet informally in the hallways. And every time we get together, the conversation quickly turns to "skill development." Time and time again, these experts have found that the majority of couples could significantly improve their marriage by simply learning one new skill for better handling their major deficiency. Research backs it up and practice bears it out: We all need new skills to make marriage work well.

The couple who is in perpetual conflict, for example, could learn how to replace criticism with complaining (a radically helpful substitution that few couples know about), and it would reduce their number of fights. The couple who mismanages money could learn to implement a budget that would reduce their debt and help them gain control. The couple whose sex life is barely breathing could learn how who takes the lead, husband or wife, and how they do it is critical to reviving their sexual pleasure. The point is that for every deficiency, there is a new skill that can improve it. Unfortunately, many couples are too complacent to make the effort that is required to learn and practice a new skill—even if it would make a world of difference.

The "X-Y-Z Formula" is a quick example. We have taught this to literally thousands of couples. Just last week, we worked with a couple who was running into problems because every little criticism either of them made of the other resulted in a huge fight. She would say something critical (and often sarcastic) about his driving, for example, and he'd get angry. Or, he would say something demeaning to her about wasting time getting ready in the mornings, and she would end up sulking. Once they learned the X-Y-Z Formula, however, all that changed. Here's how it works: In situation X, when you do Y, I feel Z. So instead of making a critical comment about his driving, she learned to say, "When we are driving down 4th Street with the kids in the back and you speed up to make the light, I sometimes feel like making the light is more important to you than our safety." This simple way

> To say the truth, reason and love keep little company together now-a-days.
> *William Shakespeare*

of phrasing a complaint is far less likely to cause problems than saying, "You are such a reckless driver!" In situation X, when you do Y, I feel Z. There are literally dozens and dozens of communication skills and techniques like this one that couples can use to fill their marital toolbox.

You may be thinking that you don't have any deficiencies. If so, that's probably your biggest deficiency! Let's make this plain and simple. Adjusting unmet expectations does not keep marital deficiency at bay. Nor does exploring the unexamined self. Like we've already said, *every* marriage has a deficiency. It may be different for every couple, but be assured that every couple has one. What every marriage doesn't necessarily have is the skill required to overcome the deficiency. That's why this third reason for problems happening to good marriages may be the most common reason of all.

So, if you feel this reason is especially relevant to your marriage, don't worry. You can be assured that in later chapters we are going to give you some of the most important new skills you need for making your marriage work in spite of what you are lacking.

Reason Four: Unhealthy Choices

Listen to these words: "We stand at the crossroads, each minute, each hour, each day, making choices. We choose the thoughts we allow ourselves to think, the passions we allow ourselves to feel, and the actions we allow ourselves to perform. Each choice is made in the context of whatever value system we've selected to govern our lives. In selecting that value system, we are, in a very real way, making the most important choice we will ever make." Benjamin Franklin said this, and his words have more wisdom for married couples than he probably ever knew.

The choices we make form the rudder that directs our marriage journey. Good choices keep us sailing smoothly in the right direction. Bad choices steer us toward the rocks. And every day in every marriage, choices are made that keep couples headed where they want to go or lead them to places that they dread.

It is difficult to exaggerate how powerful our choices are, even the small ones, in determining our path to the future. A legendary story of a man in the railroad station in St. Louis illustrates the point. He accidentally moved a small piece of railroad track a mere three inches. As a result, the train that was supposed to arrive in Newark, New Jersey, ended up in a station in New Orleans, Louisiana, some thirteen hundred miles away from its intended destination. Apocryphal or not, the illustration makes it clear: We choose our destiny.

That's why unhealthy choices are one of the leading causes of difficulty in marriage. Here are a few examples of poor choices good couples make:

- A wife who chooses to keep information from her husband about the money she spent with a girlfriend on a recent shopping spree.

- A husband who knows his work schedule is interfering with his marriage, yet chooses to work at the same pace because his job "demands it."

- A wife who chooses to use sex with her husband as a reward system rather than an expression of passion.

- A husband who chooses to keep his wife in the dark about the debt that is accruing on their credit cards.

- A wife who chooses to confess things about her marriage to her mother when she knows her husband would be infuriated.

- A husband who chooses to be with his buddies who are likely to get him into morally compromising situations he will regret.

- A wife who chooses not to give her honest opinion when her husband asks for input on his career.

- A husband who chooses to indulge a bad health habit in spite of numerous warnings from his doctor.

- A couple who chooses not to get the counseling help they need for their marriage or for themselves when they know it is needed.

Regardless of how insignificant a choice may seem at the moment, it is bound to direct our steps toward something that either enriches or diminishes our relationship. Marriage is filled with hundreds of crossroads each week, and when we choose the road less traveled, we are almost guaranteed to run into fewer bad things.

Once again, we will delve into the solutions for recovery from bad choices in other chapters—especially chapters five and six. For now we ask that you take a moment to consider some of the choices you have made that impacted your marriage by completing exercise six in the workbooks.

Exercise 6: So Many Choices

One of the best things a couple can do from time to time is review the choices they made, both good and bad, that have shaped the current state of their relationship. By examining these choices we gain power to make more constructive ones that will build a stronger union. This exercise in the workbook will help you do just that.

Reason Five: Unpredictable Circumstances

A couple may have resolved all their unrealistic expectations. They may have invited feedback and opened up themselves to their partner. They may have learned the skills required for overcoming their biggest marital deficiency. And, by the grace of God, they may have steered clear of making unhealthy choices. They may have done everything right. But this does not protect their good marriage from everything, because some bad things strike a marriage like a lightning bolt at high noon. When you least expect it, something can happen that turns your marriage, not to mention your world, inside out.

I (Les) will never forget the look on Ray's face the day he poked his head in my doorway at work and asked to talk. As colleagues at the same university, we'd known each other long enough for me to immediately see something was wrong. He walked in, shut the door, and told me his sixteen-year-old daughter, Liz, had run away from home. He was so ashamed that it took him nearly two days before he called the police. "Nancy and I are numb," he confided. "We don't know how to feel . . . enraged, depressed, frantic?" His lower lip started to quiver as my heart sank in anguish.

"How are you and Nancy holding up?" I asked.

"She won't even talk to me," Ray broke down, shoulders shuddering, tears flowing. "The night before Lizzy left, we had a run-in because she didn't like me setting her curfew. I was so upset I moved it up an hour just to spite her." Ray was trying to control his crying as I handed him a box of tissues.

"So Nancy thinks you caused Liz to run away?" I asked.

Ray defended his wife's reaction and berated himself with unflinching guilt. I tried my best to console my friend and colleague that day, but felt about as helpful as a Band-Aid on a gaping wound.

Another day passed before Liz returned safely home after hiding out with a friend whose parents were out of town. Ray and Nancy were, to say the least, relieved. They hoped life would soon get back to normal, but it didn't. As weeks turned into months, Liz's

> It takes two flints to make a fire.
> *Louisa May Alcott*

acting-out subsided, but Ray and Nancy, normally very close, began drifting apart. So much so, they got scared. That's when Ray stopped by my office again, this time to get a counseling referral for a marriage therapist. I'm happy to say they got the help they needed and worked through the issues that their family crisis stirred up between them. Not all couples who run into ugly, unpredictable circumstances are so fortunate. We all know couples who are jolted by something bad, and it shatters their good marriage forever.

Life is filled with more than enough circumstances that test a couple's strength: an employment crisis, a serious injury, the divorce of a close friend, a natural disaster, a community tragedy caused by crime, substance abuse, infertility, a rebellious son or daughter, financial loss, life-threatening illness, burglary or theft, a drunk-driving crash, an unfaithful spouse—the list goes on. Life is chock-full of bad situations that are beyond our control. And while some couples seem to control their response to these negative things better than others, few of us can avoid encountering them at some point in our journey.

For some couples, life's unpredictability is the primary reason their marriage runs headfirst into problems. When they least expected it, something hit them like a fist under the ribs and knocked the wind right out of their marriage. And who of us can judge the impact it has on their relationship?

We devoted chapter six of this book to finding solutions for such jolting experiences that far too many of us have experienced.

So Far, So Good?

No doubt you can think of other reasons problems happen to good marriages. But this list of five provides reasons enough: unfulfilled expectations, unexamined selves, unskilled couples, unhealthy choices, and unpredictable circumstances.

Maybe from this list you can immediately identify the main reason your marriage might be vulnerable. Perhaps you realize you are still holding onto unrealistic expectations that are keeping you from finding fulfillment. Maybe you recognize the need to do some serious soul-searching of ways you militantly guard your heart as a husband or a wife, or ways you hide who you are from your partner. Maybe, like so many others, you see that things might interfere with your marriage because of unhealthy choices. And if you've been hit in the gut with an ugly circumstance beyond your control, you don't need anyone to tell you that your marriage has been jolted.

Maybe one of these fits you more than the others, or maybe none of them fit you at all. Whatever the reasons, we devoted the rest of this book to helping you make the best of a good marriage—even when problems hit home.

For Reflection

1. Do you agree that these five reasons—unfulfilled expectations, unexamined selves, unskilled couples, unhealthy choices, and unpredictable circumstances—are the primary causes of negative things happening to marriages? What other reasons might you add?
2. What unrealistic expectations do you hold onto that may bring difficulty to your marriage? How have these expectations changed over the years of your relationship?
3. Have you identified your primary marital deficiency? What is it, and what are you doing to make it less of a problem?
4. Almost everyone makes unhealthy choices that impact their marriage. Looking back over your relationship, what choices do you wish you could redo and why?

Two roads diverged in a wood, and I—
I took the one less traveled by,
And that has made all the difference.
Robert Frost

tackle this problem first . . .
and all others get easier

A fine line separates an obstacle from an opportunity
and it's discovered the instant a couple sees it with new eyes.

What is the difference between an obstacle and an opportunity?
Our attitude toward it. Every opportunity has a difficulty
and every difficulty has an opportunity.
J. Sidlow Baxter

It was the best wedding reception we've ever attended. Everyone there, all one hundred–plus guests, is still talking about it, years later. The tenderloin of beef was cooked to perfection. The cake and pastries were as tasty as they were gorgeous. The flowers were beautiful. The twelve-piece orchestra was outstanding, as was the dramatic panoramic view from the hotel ballroom. Everything seemed perfect. The only thing missing was the wedding.

One week earlier the bride backed out. There was no catastrophe, no dark secrets revealed. She simply wanted to put off the wedding for a while to be sure she was doing the right thing. The groom agreed, reluctantly. And as they were calling the photographer, the church singers, and others to cancel the ceremony, they discovered it was too late to cancel the flowers or the orchestra. So the couple, along with the bride's parents, made a move that may be among the grandest in all weddingdom. They

53

had the reception anyway. Guests were notified ahead of time that the wedding was canceled, but the party wasn't.

> I am convinced that life is 10 percent what happens to me and 90 percent how I react to it. And so it is with you—we are in charge of our attitudes.
>
> *Chuck Swindoll*

The event was typical of any elegant wedding reception except the mother of the bride, who had a good sense of humor, ordered new napkins with the inscription "Murphy's Law Defied," and the bash went off without further hitches of any sort.

Some guests couldn't contain their questioning about the mother's message on the napkins. "Shouldn't it say 'Murphy's Law Defined'?" some asked. Others found the inscription delightful, a celebration of making the best of a bad situation. The difference in opinion had to do with one's attitude. What some people saw as a definition of everything going wrong, others saw as a stance against it.

Attitude. It can make a world of difference in how two people view the same thing, especially in marriage. What one of us sees as troubling, the other may see as exciting—the only difference is attitude. And few things are more toxic to a couple than a bad attitude that pervades a good marriage. For this reason, we dedicate an entire chapter to this one problem that every marriage can improve.

How can we be so bold as to say that every couple needs to improve their attitude quotient? Because attitudes impact every single marriage problem a couple ever encounters. No matter what deficiency, difficulty, or crisis a couple is trying to cope with, their attitudes will permeate the problem and either make it better or make it worse. It is no exaggeration to say that your attitude can make or break the quality of your marriage.

We begin by underscoring, as clearly as possible, how undeniably powerful attitudes are to a marriage. We show you how your attitude is your most important marital asset—how it can move you beyond your most challenging set of circumstances. Next, we walk you step-by-step toward cultivating a winning attitude, even if it feels like your marriage is not. Finally, we reveal the sure sign, the most defining fruit, of a positive attitude in marriage.

Your Most Important Marital Asset

"Isn't that the truth?" Leslie asked as we sat quietly in our car waiting for the light to turn. She was referring to the bumper sticker on the car ahead of us. It read: "Misery is an option."

And it is. If you are miserable today, you can probably point to a set of circumstances that made you so. And you may be justified in your miserable feelings. But, at the risk of sounding brash, you'd be wrong. Your circumstances didn't cause you nearly as much misery as the attitude you chose in response to them.

"The longer I live, the more I realize the impact of attitude on life," writes pastor Chuck Swindoll. "Attitude, to me, is more important than facts. It is more important than the past, than education, than money, than circumstances, than failures, than successes, than what other people think or say or do. It is more important than appearance, giftedness, or skill." He goes on to say that the most remarkable thing about life is that we can choose our attitude every day of the year. "We cannot change our past," he says. "Nor can we change the fact that people will act in a certain way. We also cannot change the inevitable." He then makes this remarkable statement: "The only thing we can do is play on the one string we have, and that is our attitude."[1]

> People are just about as happy as they make up their minds to be.
>
> *Abraham Lincoln*

Happy couples don't have a certain set of circumstances, they have a certain set of attitudes. It's tempting, no doubt, to complain about our circumstances—or our partner—when they aren't what we want, but our complaining only makes matters worse. No one has ever heard a couple say, "We hit a real turning point in our relationship once we learned to complain and blame each other." Your destiny as a couple is determined, not by your complaining, but by your decision as two individuals to rise above whatever it is you are tempted to complain about, even if it is each other.

One of the most inspirational life stories I've ever encountered is that of concentration camp survivor Viktor Frankl. I (Les) read his story for the first time when I was in college. In spite of unspeakable mistreatment by Hitler's Gestapo, Frankl made a statement that has stuck with me to this day: "The one thing you cannot take away from me is the way I choose to respond to what you do to me. The last of one's freedoms is to choose one's attitude in any given circumstance."[2] If this is true in the misery of Frankl's ungodly condition, it is certainly true in the worst misery marriage has to dish out. No one can take away our freedom to choose our attitude—no matter what our circumstances. That's why misery, especially in marriage, is an option.

Exercise 7: Your Attitude Quotient

Have you ever measured your attitude? Do people say you have a mostly positive or a mostly negative attitude? What about your spouse? This exercise in the workbooks will help both of you determine your attitude quotient. Why is this important? Because once you know what kind of attitude you tend to have, you have the opportunity to change it. Awareness is the first step in making any productive change.

What a Good Attitude Can Do for a Marriage

It is no accident that some couples live harmonious and happy lives together while others, who live in the same neighborhood, with similar financial resources, attending the same church, live in a marriage that is marked by discord and difficulty. It is no accident that some couples seem to take all life hands them in stride, rising above heartaches, while others who have had similar disadvantages are dominated by feelings of blame and resentment. It is no accident that some couples keep a good thing going in marriage while others wonder if it's worth the effort.

The reason for the discrepancy is not luck, be it good or bad. It is not their problem-solving proficiency or their skillfulness in communication, as important as these are. The reason some couples make the most of marriage while others barely make it at all is attitude, of course.

If you want to know the makings of an attitude for a miserable marriage, Murphy's Law sums it up succinctly: "Nothing is as easy as it looks; everything takes longer than you expect; and if anything can go wrong, it will and at the worst possible moment."

Happy couples live by another law: "Nothing is as hard as it looks; everything is more rewarding than you expect; and if anything can go right, it will and at the best possible moment."

If this sounds overly optimistic, it's because it is. Good attitudes open the double doors of marriage for optimism to do its work. Optimism, you see, creates opportunities and solutions we normally don't notice. Without optimism, couples see no way out of their negative circumstances. *My spouse will never change*, they say. *We've tried everything and it doesn't help.* Without optimism, even good couples consider their situations as hopeless and eventually give up.

Once in a while couples come to our counseling offices with a decision for divorce already determined. They are headed to divorce court and are just stopping by our place along the way, or so it seems. Their motivation for therapy is usually focused on how to break the news to their children, and they usually explain their situation to us something like this: "We aren't ending our marriage with a lot of hard feelings; we simply discovered that we no longer had anything in common. I guess we grew apart."

We wince each time we hear this, for it has got to be the lamest excuse possible for ending a marriage. Why? Because the way it is described, it sounds as if a divorce were inevitable—as if something in their personalities destined them to gradually separate. But we all grow in the directions we choose, and if our mate's trajectory is different from ours, it need not be the end of the relationship. It simply calls for some intentional adaptation. "Drifting apart" is an excuse for not wanting to realign our attitudes and actions with those of our partner.

An enduring marriage requires possibility thinking, elasticity, and resilience. It needs continual attention and adaptation. It requires a shift in interests as our partner's interests shift. Marriage, to remain good, involves a lifelong project of adjusting and readjusting our attitudes. For this is the only path to finding positive options to our most perplexing circumstances.

Why We Find What We're Looking For

Once a year we teach a course on marriage to undergraduates at our university. Soon into the semester we give them a simple exercise to demonstrate a simple fact about attitudes. "Look around the classroom and show the person sitting next to you everything you can find that's the color green in this room." The class is immediately abuzz with chatter. "Okay," we interrupt. "How many of you came into this room looking for green things before this exercise?" No hands go up, and a few students snicker. "What we have done, in only a few seconds, is given you a 'green mind-set.'" We go on to tell them that all of us see whatever it is we prepare our minds to see.

This fact was demonstrated beautifully in a double-blind experiment conducted at a school in the San Francisco Bay area where the principal called three teachers together and said, "Because you three teachers are the finest in the system and have the greatest expertise, we're going to give you ninety high-IQ students. We're going to let you move these students through this next year at their own pace and see how much they can learn."[3]

> You are only one thought away from a good feeling.
> *Sheila Krystal*

Both the faculty and the students were delighted and thoroughly enjoyed themselves through the entire school year. The instructors were teaching the brightest students; the students were benefiting from the close attention and instruction of highly skilled teachers. By the end of the experiment, the students had achieved 20 to 30 percent more than the other students in the entire city. That's when the principal revealed to the teachers that they did not have ninety of the most intellectually prominent students. They were random students from the system chosen to be part of an experiment.

"This means we were exceptional teachers," the instructors said.

The principal continued, "I have another confession. You're not the brightest of the teachers. Your names were the first three names drawn out of a hat."

So why did ninety students perform at such exceptional levels for an entire year? Simply because of perception. Our perception, how we view a situation, is the result of our attitude. Once we have a particular mind-set, we see everything and everybody in a certain way—either more positively or more negatively—even if our perception isn't accurate. That's why in marriage and in life, we so often find what we're looking for.

If you think your spouse is lazy, you can find plenty of evidence to support your case. If you think your spouse is efficient, you can find experiences to back that up too. Whatever you have it in your mind to find, you will.

Not long ago I was convinced Leslie had taken a fifty-dollar bill from my wallet. I was certain, because I took special care to place it at the back of my other bills earlier in the week when I went to the bank. And now it wasn't there. "I didn't touch your wallet," she protested. But during the entire afternoon everything she did seemed suspicious—the tone of her voice, her gestures. I was convinced she had taken the money and probably forgot. By the look in her eye, I sensed that even she was uncertain. But that changed in an instant when I suddenly recalled using the bill two days earlier when paying for groceries. A mind-set is a powerful thing.

> All that you achieve and all that you fail to achieve is the direct result of your own thoughts.
> *James Allen*

Some miserable people find a problem in every solution. "Yes, but ..." is their common refrain, especially in marriage therapy. "Have you tried reflecting your partner's feelings before you try to make your point in a conversation?" we might ask. "Yes, but that doesn't work because he doesn't listen to me," the client responds. "Have you considered trying to understand him before getting him to understand you?" we say in another attempt. "Yes, but he doesn't talk to me." One of the reasons some people can't find a solution to their problems is that they aren't looking for one. They've developed a mind-set, in fact, that filters solutions out.

Husbands and wives around the world are divided into two camps when it comes to their attitudes: those who have a positive mind-set and those who have a negative mind-set. By force of habit, each of us is either basically positive or basically negative. The negative person defends his attitudes with the rationale of being realistic, while the positive person looks beyond the current state of affairs and sees people and situations in terms of possibilities. The choice is theirs, or should we say *yours*.

If you are wanting to do what you can to fall into the positive attitude camp, and we believe you are, you will need to learn how to change a negative mind-set. You will need to open your eyes to things you probably haven't been looking for.

Exercise 8: What Have You Been Looking For?

What is your marriage mind-set? Do you tend to view your partner in mostly positive or mostly negative terms? This exercise in your workbooks will help you pinpoint the filters you use in viewing your spouse. It will also help you discover when you are likely to be most negative and what you can do to change that.

How to Change a Bad Attitude

Many years ago I (Les) sat in the ballroom of a hotel in Los Angeles to hear the great Rutgers anthropologist Ashley Montagu speak. His topic for the day was "psychosclerosis." It was his term for *hardening of the attitudes*. His point was fundamental: We are not born with bad attitudes. They are developed in our mind, and with effort, we can inoculate ourselves against the disease of chronic negative attitudes. While there is certainly no simple procedure for eradicating this ailment, Montagu's speech became the catalyst for us trying to develop ways to avoid it. We offer the following four steps, which have proven effective for many couples who want to turn a negative attitude around.

Step 1: Look for the Positive

This amazingly simple step can be revolutionary for some couples. It involves trying on a new mind-set, one that looks for good things about your partner and positive solutions for your predicaments. As we have already learned, each of us sees whatever we have prepared our mind to see. This step, then, becomes vital to changing a bad attitude.

Steve was convinced that his wife, Nancy, was never on time for anything. It was a major point of contention between them. So infuriating was Nancy's tardiness, that Steve would often lose his temper because of it. Nancy agreed that she sometimes did run behind schedule compared to her husband. "But he thinks he's late if he's not five minutes early," she said.

We gave these two a challenge. "For one week, lay off the accusations," we said, "and look for times your personal clocks are in synch." They did. If Steve felt his wife was going to make them late, he refrained from saying so And lo and behold, he began to notice Nancy wasn't as slow as he thought. Though she didn't operate according to his compulsive timetable, Steve began to see that Nancy was more punctual than he thought. This week-long exercise was enough for Steve to see that his desires were sometimes unreason-able and that he too often carried his fastidiousness home from work.

> Thinking is the grand originator of our experience.
> *William James*

If you have a negative attitude you can't seem to shake, you've created a convincing mind-set. Maybe you see your spouse as flir-tatious, sloppy, selfish, argumentative, or insensitive. Whatever the negative trait, the idea is to look beyond it. See if you are wearing blinders that prevent you from seeing his or her more positive qualities that balance out the negative ones. See if your mind-set is making one bad quality worse than it really is.

Step 2: Refuse to Be a Victim

In a study of individuals who survived severe physical ordeals, such as polar explorers lost in the Arctic, researchers found that they shared an implicit belief in their power to take destiny in their own hands.[4] They did not doubt that their own resources gave them the freedom to determine their fates.

The same is true for everyone who transforms a negative atti-tude resulting from an undeserved situation. Perhaps you're feel-ing sorry for yourself because you don't have the financial resources your friends do. Or maybe you didn't grow up in a home that provided good role models for marriage. Or maybe you or your partner has been laid off. Or maybe you have a physical illness that gives you every right to feel sorry for yourself. Whatever your situation, no matter how tough, you will gain nothing by being a victim.

Self-pity is the luxury no marriage can afford. It's guaranteed to drain all the energy from you and your relationship. Any amount of self-pity is more than enough.

Lisa played the victim to the hilt. Her affliction? She married too young. Anytime she and her husband hit a snag, she shook her head in shame and muttered something about being too naive to get married. In one millisecond Lisa could choose to snap out of her self-loathing if she desired. But she never seemed to think it was worth the effort. Don't allow self-pity to sabotage your attitude. Choose to step out of the victim role and determine your destiny.

Step 3: Give Up Grudges

Clara Barton, the founder of the American Red Cross, is a terrific example of someone who put this third step into practice. She was never known to hold a grudge against anyone. One time a friend recounted to her a cruel accusation that someone had fabricated against her some years earlier, but Clara seemed not to remember the incident. "Don't you remember the wrong that was done to you?" the friend asked. "No," Clara answered calmly. "I distinctly remember forgetting that."

Nothing keeps good attitudes from emerging more than a good grudge. Bitterness and resentment are the poisons of positive thinking. So in your desire to build a better attitude, it is essential to follow Clara Barton's example and give up your grudges, no matter how well justified they seem.

Melinda, a woman in her early forties, held on to a grudge against her husband, Walt, for so long she could barely remember when it started. "Somewhere early in our marriage," she told us, "Walt decided to go to a football game with his friends instead of a Sunday dinner with my parents." You could still feel the anger in her voice and see the resentment in her face, all these years later. "Ever since then, I could give you hundreds of examples of how Walt's games are more important than me." In a counseling session with us, Walt protested her accusation, but to no avail. Melinda was dead set on holding on to a grudge that had sunk its bitter roots deep into their marriage. The grudge prevented her from seeing any alternatives to her negative, closed-case mind-set. But in time, with the help of several counseling sessions, Melinda eventually began to get the chip off her shoulder and look beyond her grudge. Little by little, as the resentment melted, Melinda gave Walt the space to prove his love for her.

> The supreme happiness of life is the conviction of being loved for yourself, or, more correctly, of being loved in spite of yourself.
>
> *Victor Hugo*

This can be a frightening prospect, for sure. Maybe you feel your spouse's lack of affection is ruining your marriage. Perhaps you've never forgiven him or her for an embarrassing and ugly outburst. Maybe your resentment has nothing to do with your marriage directly but stems from your childhood or home life. Whatever the cause, bitterness clogs the veins of a positive attitude, and it must be expelled in order to give life to good thoughts.

Step 4: Give Yourself and Your Marriage Some Grace

In the Canadian northlands there are just two seasons, winter and July. When the back roads begin to thaw, they become so muddy that vehicles going into the backwoods country leave deep ruts that become frozen when cold weather returns. For those entering this primitive area during the winter months, there is a sign which reads, "Driver, please choose carefully which rut you drive in, because you'll be in it for the next twenty miles."

Some negative attitudes are so habit-forming they become like frozen ruts, and we can easily find ourselves in them twenty years down the road. It takes serious effort to change these negative thinking patterns, to take the steps we outline in this chapter, and so we urge you to give yourself and your partner grace along the way. If your attitude change isn't as quick or as consistent as you'd like, go easy on yourself. Remember that each new day presents another opportunity to start fresh. And each day that you make this effort to improve your attitude brings you closer to the marriage you desire.

> What lies behind us and what lies before us are tiny matters compared to what lies within us.
>
> *Walt Emerson*

Think of it this way. When an airplane travels toward a destination, it is actually off course most of the time. However, the computers on board are constantly correcting its path, bringing it back into alignment with the destination. In the same way, your alterations to your attitude may not always be exactly on target, but that does not mean you are not headed in the right direction. So give yourself grace, and don't give up when you momentarily veer off course.

Real-Life Problem Solvers

How We Won over a Bad Attitude

Kevin and Kathy Lunn
Married in 1989

When we got married, I knew Kevin's job as a management consultant meant he would be on the road and away from home from time to time. That was okay with me. If he were ever to make partner at his firm someday, he had to pay his dues. What wasn't okay with me was the resentment I felt as the years rolled along. His traveling was taking him away from me, at times, for nearly the whole week. I was beginning to feel like our home was just another hotel stop over the weekend. *Why can't we be like other couples with normal schedules?* I whined. *Why is he doing this to me?*

I (Kevin) didn't understand Kathy's complaining. She seemed to exaggerate the number of days I was gone and never valued how hard I was working to support us. Eventually, my resentment began to mount, too. *I'm breaking my back*, I thought, *and all she thinks I do is have fancy dinners with clients.* We were both feeling like victims, captives of our own negative thinking.

Kevin's Experience

Once I made partner, I had more control over my schedule than ever. I was on the road most weeks, but my trips were much briefer. Besides, it wasn't like I wanted to be out of town. I lived for the days I was at home with Kathy and our baby, Meg. And on the days I was gone, I'd always call to check in and connect with Kathy. But more often than not, our phone conversations eventually turned negative. If the car broke down, for example, she wanted me to fix it—no matter that I was in Phoenix, St. Louis, or Seattle. I resented being blamed for problems beyond my control, especially when I was working so hard. *If she would only be more supportive*, I thought to myself, *everything would be just fine.*

Kathy's Experience

While Kevin's world was getting bigger, mine was getting smaller. He was traveling all over the country, while I was stuck at home. I was left to fend for myself when the base-

ment flooded, when the batteries went out in the smoke
alarm, when the driveway needed to be shoveled after a
heavy snow, when the car needed maintenance, and anything else that most wives manage with help from their
husbands. I resented that. I grew up in a home where Dad,
a farmer, took care of almost everything. What I resented
most, however, was Kevin's schedule. Because he was
often in a different time zone while traveling and manag-
ing a jam-packed day, I could never talk to him when I
wanted. It was his schedule that took precedence, not
mine. I planned my days around Kevin's nightly phone
calls. And because of that, my attitude could not have
been more sour.

How We Solved the Problem

Our solution can be found in one primary word: attitude.
Within the last couple years we both came to a very humble place and recognized how our negative thinking was
preventing us from doing anything constructive to make
our marriage better. Sure, we had some practical challenges that not every couple faces, but it was nothing we
couldn't contend with once we individually owned our
bad attitudes. For us, that meant taking responsibility for
how we approached our problem rather than blaming the
other person and playing the role of the victim. I'd like
my husband to be home every day of the week, but he
makes part of his living on the road, and he's good at
what he does. Truth is, I'm proud of him. And he's proud
of me. He's told me how much he admires how well I
manage our home while he's away.

Once we discarded our negative thinking, we began to
see each other's contributions to our marriage more
clearly. Today, we have found little ways to make the long-
distance trips easier. Knowing that I need to call whenever

I want, for example, Kevin has made my calls to his cell phone (thanks to "caller ID") a top priority. At last, we are coping with the situation successfully. And that would never have been possible if we had not *decided* to change our negative attitudes.

A Word to Other Couples

Negative thinking is a luxury you cannot afford if you want to build the marriage of your dreams.

The Sure Sign of a Positive Marriage Attitude

Last year I (Les) traveled for four days with my seventy-five-year-old father to Rome, Italy. While he had been to Rome on previous occasions, it was my first visit. With little time to spare, we made a list of places we wanted to see, hired a driver, and immersed ourselves in the city. Our first stop was the Vatican, where we toured St. Peter's and the Sistine Chapel. We visited the Coliseum and the catacombs where the early Christians secretly worshiped. We made a special trip to the prison cell where the apostle Paul wrote so many letters now found in the New Testament.

One night as we enjoyed a spaghetti dinner in the dining room of our hotel, we got to talking about a biblical principle I had never fully understood. It had to do with a law the Roman Empire established that required boys in villages to carry Roman soldiers' backpacks one mile from their home. Because the practice of this law was so pervasive, smart kids would measure a mile down the road in both directions from their house and drive a stake in the ground to mark the distance. That way they knew exactly how far they would need to carry a soldier's pack. They could set the pack on the other side of the stake and thus fulfill the letter of the law.

When Jesus preached his Sermon on the Mount, he used this Roman practice as an illustration for how a person can improve his or her relationships. Jesus said this: "If someone forces you to go one mile, go with him two miles" (Matthew 5:41). A couple who practices this powerful extra-mile principle is, in our opinion, guaranteed to enjoy the fruits of a strong marriage.

Almost everybody walks the first mile in marriage. That's the mile that takes out the trash or prepares the nightly dinner. The extra mile, however, does the same mundane chores with a kind spirit and a smile. Not every husband or wife does that. In fact, most of us live in one-mile marriages. But when attitudes improve, you are sure to witness the extra-mile principle at work.

> We don't see things as they are, we see them as we are.
> *Anais Nin*

All of us have the wide-open option of choosing the way we will live in a marriage. The pattern of behavior we develop in this relationship may stem from the home we grew up in, the education we have, and numerous other conditions, but the attitudes we finally choose to live by are our own. That is precisely why a bad attitude is the one bad thing every good marriage can make better.

For Reflection

1. As you survey the landscape of your marriage, what kinds of attitudes do you see? If you are like most couples, you could probably use an attitude tune-up. If so, what single attitudes do you need to change the most?
2. When it comes to changing a bad attitude, one of the first things experts recommend is to change your mind-set by looking for the positive. What positive things have you recently been overlooking in your relationship?
3. In what ways have you allowed self-pity to infiltrate your marriage? Have either of you played the self-loathing victim? If so, what are the results?
4. What do you think of the "extra-mile principle" in marriage? Do you agree that it is a good barometer of positive attitudes that both of you bring to your relationship? Why?

Married life can never be what it ought to be
while the husband or wife makes
personal happiness the main object.
J. S. Kirtley

---

who said sex was a problem?

The magic of marriage inevitably wanes if you don't recognize and accept the two sides of intimacy and sex (not to mention having a baby).

Change, whether negative or positive, can shake up a relationship.
Norman Epstein

Last night we returned home from a Hawaiian vacation. It was our first major getaway, just the two of us, in two years— since our baby was born. We'd planned and anticipated this trip for nearly a year. Every detail, including reservations for a convertible rental car and a room at a beachside hotel, was nailed down. Our bags were packed with swimsuits, sunglasses, and sunscreen. We could almost taste the pineapple and papaya, hear the melodic island music, and feel the warm tropical breeze before the wheels of our jetliner lifted off the runway in our rainy city of Seattle. Good-bye winter; we were headed for paradise. Or so we thought.

With a single word, the pilot changed the course of our vacation before we had even landed in Hawaii: "Rain." A massive cold front was moving over the islands, and that meant rain. Not the kind that lightly sprinkles the Hawaiian shores for a few minutes in the afternoon. Not even the kind that slowly drains the overcast skies of the Pacific Northwest for hours at a time. We arrived in Hawaii for one of the worst continual torrential downpours they'd seen in months. The kind of rain that causes flash floods and serious road closures, not to mention serious disappointment.

"Look at this," Les said, holding up a sheet of paper that was surreptitiously slid under the door of our hotel room shortly after we checked in. "It says here we're not supposed to leave the premises because of flood warnings."

"You're kidding me," I said helplessly.

"And," he continued in amazement, "they are closing the main restaurant because the weather prevented food deliveries."

What?! This can't be happening, I said to myself. *What about our exciting excursions? Our romantic dinners? What about sunshine and happiness in paradise?*

That evening as we sat in our room clicking through the local TV news reports while eating overpriced candy bars from the hotel minibar, I think I understood what author Eric Hoffer meant when he said, "Disappointment is a sort of bankruptcy— the bankruptcy of a soul that expends too much in expectation." All our expectations and our money were literally going down the drain. Our excitement was slipping away. We felt bankrupt.

It never entered our minds that this trip would turn out the way it did. Everything we anticipated was thrown into reverse. Disappointment derailed our fun. We tried to make the best of a not-so-good situation (we'll never forget laughing hysterically while swimming in the pouring rain), but this good idea turned bad before it even started.

The whole thing was a kind of a microcosm of our marriage. Not all of it, but the parts that don't

> We promised to work to stay together not because we think things between us will never change, but because we know they will.
>
> *Eric Zorn*

turn out the way we want. Every marriage, in fact, encounters good things that go bad. Like a spoiled vacation, some disappointments strike at the most unpredictable times and in the least likely places. We find ourselves in conditions that are supposed to be good and wonder why they aren't. That's what compounds the disappointment and compels us to examine our marriage to see if it, and not just our circumstances, have turned terribly bad.

Here we will take a look at three of the most predictable conditions of marriage that cause some couples to draw inaccurate conclusions about the state of their relationship only because of their disappointing circumstances. We look first at how the intimacy we've always wanted can sometimes become an invasion of privacy. We then turn our attention to how the miracle of a new baby can take the magic out of marriage. And we conclude with a look at how sex in marriage can become seemingly nonexistent.

Like a fruit that has become too ripe, each of these situations started out good and, for a variety of reasons, turned bad. We're not as interested in the reasons, however, as much as we are the solutions. So here are the three most common things that can go bad for some couples.

When Intimacy Becomes Invasion

"By marrying," Robert Louis Stevenson warned, "you have willfully introduced a witness into your life ... and can no longer close the mind's eye upon uncomely passages, but must stand up straight and put a name upon your actions." Why? Because if you don't, your partner will.

Marriage is the closest bond that is possible between two people. Legally, socially, emotionally, physically, there is no other means of getting closer to another human being. It is this extraordinary closeness that propels us into matrimony. We long to belong to another person that knows us and loves us like nobody else in the world. This kind of intimacy is the rocket fuel of marriage. It is what enables couples to transcend themselves and explore the universe of love. Without intimacy, life becomes horribly cold and lonely. So we plunge ourselves into marriage and give our heart in exchange for another to discover the deepest and most radical expression of human connection possible.

Eventually, however, seasoned couples also discover that such closeness can be exhausting. It pulls our very identity into the vortex of another human life and can leave little room to breathe. Intimacy, it seems, leaves nowhere to hide. That's what Robert Louis Stevenson is getting at when he says that marriage willfully introduces a witness into our lives. Marriage causes us to submit to the humility of being known in all our phoniness and pride, in all our frailty and the blackness of our sin. And who cares, really, to be known *that* well by another person? Who wants to live under scrutiny and surveillance? And yet this is the price marriage puts on intimacy, to be put in the spotlight of our spouse.

> A good marriage is one which allows for change and growth in the individuals.
>
> *Pearl Buck*

Perhaps the most unnerving thing about marriage for some is that it sweeps away our defenses and increases the probability of pain. There is no one who can stand up to the day-in and day-out demands of intimacy and not get hurt. Whereas in most other relationships our vulnerability can be hidden or guarded at times, marriage strips us of all protection with our spouse, because he or she has been allowed into our inner sanctum. Our partner has witnessed our naked soul, by virtue of being our soul mate. That's why your spouse can see right through your masquerades and facades and read your subtlest fluctuations of mood and thought, even when you try to keep them private. And in those moments you may feel as though this intimacy has gone too far, that intimacy has become an invasion.

Marriage makes us accountable to one another, and that accountability is both the best and worst part of marriage. It keeps you sane. It also drives you crazy. So if the goodness of intimacy is at risk of turning bad in your marriage, consider the following practical suggestions.

First, note the personal information your spouse knows about you that makes you feel most vulnerable. This is the kind of information you don't want talked about with others. It is the information you don't want used against you in times of conflict. Because intimacy makes us so vulnerable to potential pain, we need to be very clear with each other that certain things are off limits (the ridicule we suffered as a child, for example, or the difficult relationship we currently have with a parent). To use them against us would be akin to hitting beneath the belt.

When intimacy becomes invasion, it is also a good idea to draw boundary lines that provide personal space. At the end of a long, stressful day, for example, you may need to acknowledge that you need time to yourself to decompress before interacting with your partner. This can be easier than you think. We have a friend who often stops by a Wal Mart store a couple days a week on his way home from work. He's not catching up on shopping; he simply finds it relaxing to stroll the aisles for a few minutes before heading home. It helps him put his mind in neutral and shift gears from a stressful workday before greeting his wife. Because he was up front with his need for space, she understands and appreciates the difference his Wal-Mart excursions make.

> We have been seamed, not grafted. Though our steps interlock, each dances his own dance.
> *Luci Shaw*

In addition to setting up boundaries that mark off personal time and personal issues, marriage can also benefit from property lines. These are the lines that tell our partner that it's okay to borrow my sweatshirt but not my toothbrush. Or, it's okay to read my magazines, but not my e-mail. If there are particular things you like to keep for yourself, anything from a roll of stamps in your desk drawer to things you keep in your purse, set a property line. This can be helpful for both partners. We know a woman who was disgusted by her husband drinking directly out of the milk carton in the refrigerator. Now he has his own clearly marked carton that nobody else touches.

In addition to these practical suggestions, we want to note a final insight that will enable you to put them into practice. *Intimacy does not demand agreement.* This is an obvious point to some, but for those who have made the mistake of this assumption, it bears stating. Some couples erroneously think that true intimacy means giving up their individuality, their own unique thoughts and feelings. This misbelief involving the blending of two identities is what led Ruth Graham, wife of evangelist Billy Graham, to say, "If we agreed on everything, there wouldn't be a need for both of us."

Genuine love always preserves a distinction between oneself and one's partner. It prizes separateness, knowing that another person can never be an extension of oneself. That's why we often ask each partner in a couple we are counseling to state the purpose and function of their spouse. When they define the purpose of their partner in reference to themselves ("she's supposed to make my dinner and keep the house clean," or "he's supposed to make a living and provide for me"), we know we have our work cut out for us in helping the couple overcome their problems. Why? Because they will need to learn that each of them has their own separate destiny to fulfill beyond being a couple. They will need to learn that the purpose and function of their spouse is to become whatever it is that God uniquely designed them to be. They will need to learn that the separateness they have not yet come to value will become the very thing that enriches their union.

Shortly after we were married and living in Los Angeles, our friend James Scott Smith gave us a collector's edition of poetry by Kahlil Gibran.[1] In it we found the famous words Gibran penned concerning the invasion of intimacy in marriage. So many years later in our own marriage these words now make much more sense.

> Let there be spaces in your togetherness,
> And let the winds of the heavens dance between you.
> Love one another, but make not a bond of love:
> Let it rather be a moving sea between the shores of your souls.
> Fill each other's cup but drink not from one cup.
> Give one another of your bread but eat not from the same loaf.
> Sing and dance together and be joyous, but let each one of you
>   be alone,
> Even as the strings of a lute are alone though they quiver with
>   the same music.

Exercise 9: Coping with the Invasion of Intimacy

Almost every husband and wife struggle with an overload of intimacy at some point—a time when either one of them feels that their own space has been swallowed up by their partner. This workbook exercise will help you identify how significant this situation is in your own marriage and direct you toward productive coping strategies for keeping intimacy from becoming an invasion.

When Babies Become a Burden

If ever there was a husband and wife ready to become mom and dad, it was Kevin and Judy. With their first baby on the way, their excitement was palpable. They prepared the nursery right down to a neatly ordered stack of diapers, signed up for Lamaze courses, and were reading all the *What to Expect* books. Late at night they would lie in bed and talk about their future with a baby. What they didn't realize was that they were not only giving birth to a new human, they were giving birth to a new marriage. Ready or not, they were about to be sucked into a huge force that would propel them through a passage where they would emerge changed. Every new mom and dad go through it.

When you have a child, you are still yourself, but now, as a mother or father, you are some new version of yourself. And you are standing in the middle of some new version of your marriage. Make no mistake about it, the birth of each child signals a serious and permanent alteration in your marriage. The alteration is, of course, deeply enriching if not miraculous, but for the majority of couples it is also somewhat confusing, if not downright challenging.

> I know some good marriages—marriages where both people are just trying to get through their days by helping each other and being good to each other.
>
> Erica Jong

Studies show that when baby makes three, conflicts increase eightfold, marriage takes a backseat, women feel overburdened, and men feel shoved aside. By the baby's first birthday, most mothers are less happy about their marriage, and some are wondering whether their marriage will even make it. Baby-induced marital meltdowns are not uncommon. With the help of researchers like John Gottman, at the University of Washington, here's what we know for sure. In the year after the first baby arrives, 70 percent of wives experience a precipitous plummet in their marital satisfaction. For the husband, the dissatisfaction usually kicks in later, as a reaction to his wife's unhappiness.[2] The problems have little to do with whether the baby is colicky or a good sleeper, or whether the mother is working or staying at home. It simply has to do with how a little addition shifts the whole dynamic within a household.

How can something as good as a little baby turn a marriage so bad? We could point to a wide range of reasons: lack of sleep, feeling overwhelmed and unappreciated, the awesome responsibility of caring for such a helpless little creature, juggling chores and other economic stress, and lack of time to oneself, among other things. The root reason, however, is no big mystery. In plain language, children take time and attention away from a marriage. They suck all the hours out of the day and fill up every spare cell in your brain. Being a parent is wonderful, only somehow, it's made being a spouse . . . different. "Before kids, I was thrilled to hear my husband's voice on the phone," said Judy, a few years into motherhood. "Now after a day of meetings and phone calls and carpools and wet swimsuits, I sometimes wonder who is this guy who seems to want food, an audience, and— he's got to be joking—sex?"

Isn't it romantic?

Of course not. But a lack of romance and connection isn't inevitable during this phase of marriage. The fact is, these are the good times, and that guy leafing through his mail oblivious to the baby's cries is your partner. That woman who used to give you back rubs and is now busy cleaning peanut butter off door handles is your soul mate. Someday you're going to look back on this period fondly—but only if both of you can keep this good thing from turning bad. The experts offer a primary suggestion: Expand your sense of "one-ness" to "we-ness" to include your children.

Motherhood brings every new mom a bassinet full of new feelings. She has never felt a love as deep and selfless as the one she feels for her child. She almost always experiences a profound new meaning in her life. She discovers she is willing to make enormous sacrifices for her child. "The experience is so life-altering," says John Gottman, "that if her husband doesn't go through it with her, it is understandable that distance would develop between them."[3] So the key to keeping a good marriage good while mom is experiencing an intensely wonderful transformation is for dad to undergo the same thing. In other words, marital success has everything to do with whether the husband experiences the transformation to parenthood along with his wife. If not, he gets left behind, pining for the old "us," while his wife is embracing a new sense of "we-ness" that includes their child.

A new father often resents how little time his wife has for him (especially in their sex life) now that they have a baby. He resents how tired she always is. He loves his child, but he wants his wife back the way she was. What's a husband to do? Get over his whining and follow her into the new realm she has entered. He has to become a father as well as a husband. He must cultivate feelings of pride, tenderness, and protectiveness for his offspring. In other words, he must see his journey into parenthood as a sign and an opportunity for significant personal growth.

> A successful marriage is not a gift, it is an achievement.
>
> *Ann Landers*

All the responsibility for navigating a marriage through the unknown channels of parenthood does not rest with the husband alone. A new mother often resents the lack of emotional romance her husband now brings to the marriage. *He's changed*, you may think. *He's more distant*. In actuality, his efforts to embrace this new "we-ness" have probably sidetracked the energy he put into your old romance. And the more stock you put in romance before the baby was born, the more loss you will feel when your busy husband seems disconnected.

If you were taught to believe that happy couples must be romantic ones, you may mourn the loss of romance way out of proportion to its worth. "But it's so little to ask," you say. "Just a bunch of flowers once in a while to let me know he remembers." If you give romance more importance than it deserves, you may become even more troubled and say, "Maybe he's lost interest in me." The problem for parents with this kind of reasoning is found in how they define romance. We tend to think of it as that knee-weakening, heart-pounding, earth-moving spasm that occurs with our spouse. But is it realistic to expect that kind of dazzle during motherhood? Maybe, but probably not to the degree you enjoyed it before kids came along. A moonlit stroll with your new husband, for example, is distinctly different from that same stroll six years later, when you've wrestled the kids to bed, the sink is filled with dirty dishes, and you still have laundry to do. Romance need not end with parenthood, but it may need to take a new form while your husband works to find his place as a father.

The bottom line? As a new mom and new dad, you each have your role in keeping a good marriage going. Dads need to work at entering their wives' new world, and moms need to give their husbands space to do so. But you both need to expand your sense of "one-ness" to "we-ness."

Real-Life Problem Solvers

HOW WE FOUND TIME AND SPACE AS A COUPLE WITH KIDS

Andrea and Chris Fabry
Married in 1982

If anyone knows what it's like to have kids change a marriage, it's us. We have eight children, ranging in ages from eight months to fifteen years of age, and sometimes it feels like we've quit being partners in order to become parents. Right from the beginning we fell into this trap. With our firstborn in 1985, the tension began to mount, especially for me (Andrea). Suddenly, Chris didn't seem to be sharing the load, and I felt like my needs and desires as a wife were becoming consumed by motherhood.

Chris's Experience

I could tell there was something wrong after our first baby, but I tried to laugh my way out of stressful situations. I would minimize any concern Andrea brought up about our marriage. I thought it was just a phase new parents went through and didn't pay it much attention. When we had a fight, I just wanted to show her I was right. The more children we had, the more intense Andrea's emotional pain became. I got to the point where I couldn't help any longer. Everything I said was wrong.

Andrea's Experience

With the birth of our first child, the ugly issues that were residing beneath the surface of our relationship became exposed. Suddenly I felt as though there was not one child in our house, but two. My husband's irresponsibility was driving me nuts. I was desperate for help to salvage my marriage. I needed time for just the two of us. I needed Chris to grow up and become a father as well as a husband. I needed relief.

How We Solved the Problem

Sweeping my marital frustrations under the rug was not working for any of us—me, Chris, or the kids. I (Andrea) entered counseling and learned a principle that turned our marriage around: I needed to stop walking on eggshells and speak my mind about my needs. So I did. I confronted my husband with my desires. I talked to Chris about finding balance in my life, about being a wife as well as a mother. I confronted him with his immaturity. I told him I felt like I was mothering him as much as our children. I told him I was getting swallowed by motherhood. I needed a teammate, an adult, a father as well as a husband.

When I (Chris) learned just how much of a jerk I was being by not carrying my fair share with the kids and our marriage, I began going to counseling with Andrea. That's when I saw our marriage situation as less "her" problem and more "our" problem. In time, I even saw much of it as "my" problem. Both of us worked together on breaking out of our unhealthy patterns of relating.

To this day, I (Andrea) continue to be aware of how I might baby my husband. I make my own needs known. And I help him be the husband he wants to be.

For the past year, I (Chris) have had a friend who has kept me accountable as a father and a husband. I also keep daily reminders on my desk, and I set aside date nights for Andrea and me to be husband and wife—not just mommy and daddy.

A Word to Other Couples

Love your children and each other enough to draw boundaries that protect your marriage.

Exercise 10: When Husband and Wife Become Mom and Dad

If you have recently experienced the marital changes that come from entering parenthood, this workbook exercise will help you put into practice the ideas we discussed in this section. It is one thing to read about the changes in a book, and quite another to apply them to your specific situation. This exercise will help you do just that.

When Sex Becomes a Thing of the Past

"Honey, are you coming to bed soon?" Robert hollered to his wife as he was climbing under the covers.

"Mmm, a little later," Cindy replied.

Translation: "Do you want to make love?" Answer: "Not a chance."

The dialogue was familiar, but this time it was edged with a quality of brooding tension that distinguished it from the hundreds of similar invitation-and-refusal scenes they'd enacted before. When Cindy finally did come to bed that night, Robert was still awake, bristling with frustration.

"Every night, it's the same routine," he snapped. "Aren't we ever going to have sex?"

Cindy marshaled her usual arguments about being exhausted after a day of chasing two small kids, but this time she stopped dead in her tracks. She was bone-weary of the years of conflict, guilt, and crushing sense of inadequacy that pervaded her lack of interest in lovemaking. She rolled over with her back to Robert, then rolled her eyes to herself and softly said, "I don't care if I ever have sex again."

From the other side of the bed, Robert lay in silence, seething with anger and frustration.

How does a marriage get to this point? It started so differently. When they began, Robert and Cindy were plenty attracted to each other. Saving sex for their wedding night only heightened their desire. Even after their marriage, they made love frequently and passionately. During those early years Robert and Cindy were about as perfectly matched on the erotic front as any couple could hope to be. So what happened? How did they end up with their sex life going AWOL?

Robert and Cindy are like countless other married couples whose sex life started out good and somehow turned bad. Sexual standoffs strike more marriages than researchers have been able to tabulate. But if you are having problems in the bedroom, little comfort is found in knowing that you're not the only one. So let's get right to the solution.

It begins by steering clear of the blame-shame cycle that sabotages so many sexually polarized couples. When one person, usually the male but not always, is more interested in lovemaking than his wife, it is easy to fall into a trap of blaming the wife for not being more motivated. And it is easy for her to feel ashamed because she's not. The screws of inadequacy get turned tighter with each occurrence of blame, no matter how subtly the blame is expressed. A woman feels unworthy for not matching the "normal" sex drive of her husband, unworthy for failing to live up to a fundamental expectation of a committed relationship, unworthy for repeatedly turning her back on her partner's fervent desire for her. And this inadequacy can be transferred to her husband, who may feel profoundly unwanted because of his wife's lack of desire

> We human beings can survive the most difficult of circumstances if we are not forced to stand alone.
> *James Dobson*

for him. That's why it's a sabotaging cycle that can only be broken when each partner admits they don't know the other's "problem"—so they can't blame each other for not conforming to their particular libido and timetable.

In more practical terms, one of the best ways to avoid the blame-shame cycle is to recognize that your sexual stalemate, in all likelihood, isn't personal. Research is revealing that biology, especially the neurochemistry that determines each person's hormonal levels, is more responsible for sexual motivation than we ever knew. So what may appear to be a sexual problem that is purely relationship-driven, probably isn't. As respected sex therapist Patricia Love says in her book *Hot Monogamy*, "It is entirely possible to love someone a lot, but still not be very sexually turned on by him or her."[4] In other words, a sexual refusal by a wife is not necessarily a way of punishing her husband. She is probably not "withholding" sex to lord it over him. It may have much more to do with her lack of testosterone. But here's the good news: Even if a person's hormonal makeup is contributing to a natural difference in libido, it is entirely possible, with sufficient time and effort, to develop a satisfying sexual connection.

Having worked on a professional level with scores of couples who suffer a substantial desire gap, and having worked on a personal level to keep passion alive in our own marriage, we understand the private misery of a couple like Robert and Cindy. And we also understand that their lovemaking will improve only when they consciously create opportunities for it. This begins when each partner shares with the other what kind of sexual-emotional activity would feel most loving and satisfying to them. For Robert it might be a periodic session of sex that gives him both a measure of physical release and the feeling that Cindy cared for him. For Cindy, it might be receiving regular, leisurely massages from her husband, which might or might not culminate in intercourse, depending on her wishes.

This discussion may reveal that your partner's desires are almost alien to your own impulses. But talking about it will gradually deepen a mutual understanding that will lead each of you to an experience of passion that is both different from your own and entirely valid (workbook exercise nine will help you do this). This is what gives couples the capacity to stretch and respond to each other's needs. We aren't saying the result will be blood-boiling sexual fireworks, but more realistically a budding sense of mutual intimacy and trust that can energize both an erotic and an emotional reconnection. It will begin a healthy process of better sex where each of you is more likely to get what you want.

Real-Life Problem Solvers

HOW WE REIGNITED OUR SEXUAL FIRE

Rick and Jennifer Newberg
Married in 1981

Our honeymoon could not have been better. Not only was our trip to the Bahamas outstanding, but so was the sex. In fact, it remained outstanding well into the first year of our marriage. We made love, on average, at least two times a week. The second year of marriage saw a slight downward trend, but while the quantity got lower, the quality increased. After three years of marriage, we had our first baby, and that's when our sex life hit a major low and only got worse. Well into the first decade of our marriage, we were barely giving a thought to our sex life, let alone doing anything about it. We had "vacation sex" once in a while and, if we were lucky, another isolated experience here or there. To say our sexual fire was beginning to fade was an understatement. It had all but burned out.

Rick's Experience

Like most guys, sex is important to me. I remember thinking during the first year of marriage that I must be the luckiest guy on earth to have such a great sex life with my wife. But once our first baby was born, it seemed to me that Jennifer lost all interest in sex. When I tried to touch her in a romantic way, she usually gave me the brush-off. If I came right out and asked her to have sex, she said I was being too pushy. I remember buying her a nice negligee that promptly went into a dresser drawer—never to appear again. On those rare occasions when we did have sex, it felt to me like Jennifer was doing me a favor. I was confused. How could something so great turn out so bad for us?

Jennifer's Experience

Once we got married, I remember being truly invested in our sex life. I wanted it to be great, not only for Rick, but for me too. We were creative in our lovemaking, and I always enjoyed it. But once we started our family, something inside me changed. All my focus and all my physical and emotional energy went into our kids. I didn't feel like I had much left over for Rick, especially in bed. I was exhausted most days, and when I had some modicum of energy left over, I didn't feel like using it to have sex. Most days I never got to read a real book or enjoy something else that was just for me. I felt guilty for not having more sex with Rick. And the longer we went without it, the tougher it was to do it.

How We Solved the Problem

About a half dozen years ago, our sex life took a major positive turn. We were on vacation, and Jennifer was reading a book about marriage. Sitting beside a pool, she asked me what I would change if I could change anything about our marriage. It didn't take me long to answer: I wanted to improve our sex life. Her question actually sparked a discussion that eventually led to a plan of action for improving our sex life. We both knew that sex was a deficit in our relationship, and for the first time in a long while I (Jennifer) wanted to make it a priority. I knew it was important to our marriage, and we were missing out on something great.

Here's what we did. First, we talked about our expectations and what each of us would like from our sex life (we got specific). Second, we literally set appointments on the calendar to share a passionate evening together. This wasn't as formal as it sounds. Our "appointments" became something we eagerly anticipated. Third, we began to enjoy spontaneous interludes every once in a while that were quick and fun (sometimes over a lunch break). Fourth, we bought a sturdy lock for our bedroom door to ensure one of our kids didn't wander in for a late-night glass of water (this was especially important to Jennifer). Fifth, we spent a little money on some exciting lingerie. And six, we read a couple of books about improving our sex life, including *52 Ways to Have Fun, Fantastic Sex* by Cliff and Joyce Penner. All of these things working together have put the fire back in our sex life for nearly twelve years running.

A Word to Other Couples

Don't be afraid to schedule times to have sex together. These may end up being the best appointments you've ever made.

Exercise 11: Refueling the Sexual Fire

Many couples would like to deepen their understanding of each other's sexuality but aren't too sure how to have a productive discussion on this topic. They have tried to talk, but their talking led to hurt feelings and further distance. If this has ever happened to you, don't be discouraged. This workbook exercise will show you how to talk about your sex life together in a way that is healthy and fruitful.

One More Thought

Well, there they are. The three most common good things in marriage that run the risk of turning bad. Before we leave this chapter, however, we feel compelled to note that its goal has not been to help you maintain a "perfect" marriage where you can always prevent good things from turning into problems. No matter what measures are taken, they will. That's part of the marriage package. You'd be hard-pressed to find a couple who expects their relationship to keep everything that's good on an even keel and problems at bay. But the whole issue begs the question we haven't yet answered: What is reasonable to expect from a marriage?

The late British psychiatrist D. W. Winnicott put forth the idea of "good-enough mothering."[5] He was convinced that mothering could never be perfect because of the mother's own emotional needs. "Good-enough mothering" refers to the imperfect, though adequate provision of emotional care that can raise a healthy child. In a similar vein, we believe there is a level of imperfection in marriage that is good enough to live and grow on. In the good-enough marriage, painful encounters and various frustrations occasionally occur, but they are balanced by the strength and pleasures of the relationship. There are enough positives, in other words, to balance the negatives. Good enough.

This standard is essentially subjective, but there is at least one common objective criteria. A marriage must have enough companionship, affection, autonomy, connectedness, and separateness for both partners to feel fulfilled. In other words, if one person is unhappy in the relationship, then by definition it is not good enough and requires work.

What's to be gained by this "good-enough" perspective? Well, couples looking for a good-enough marriage are bound to be far happier than those seeking perfection. And that is enough.

For Reflection

1. Can you think of an anticipated experience you were both looking forward to that did not turn out to be what you had hoped? What happened and how did the two of you cope with the surprising turn of events?

2. Almost every spouse knows the experience of feeling a bit smothered by his or her partner. When intimacy becomes invasion for you, what do you do to cope, and what might you do in the future to cope better?

3. If you have had a baby, how has it impacted your relationship—both for the better and for the worse? Do you think this season in marriage is something that most couples can improve, or do you think that they simply need to wait it out until their marriage finds a new equilibrium?

4. It is the rare couple who has not had struggles in their sex life. How would you rate your problems in this on a onc-to-ten scale? If it is needing some work, what is one specific thing both of you can do immediately to make it better?

Don't smother each other.
No one can grow in shade.
Leo Buscaglia

the six subtle saboteurs
of every marriage

Learn to defend your marriage against these sneak attacks
and you will have built an impenetrable fortress of love.

There is much pain that is quite noiseless;
and vibrations that make human agonies are often
a mere whisper in the roar of hurrying existence.
George Eliot

Greg and I hid under Jim's bed for nearly an hour. It was another Friday night, and I was staying over for some weekend fun. And as was our custom on such occasions, Greg and I, both about ten years old, had rolled up blankets and arranged them under the covers of our own beds to make Jim believe we were already fast asleep when he returned home. The mission was to hide out until Jim was about to crawl under his own covers—then reach out from under his bed and grab his ankles, and scream as his fifteen-year-old body went into convulsive shock. It was known by the three of us as the infamous "sleep attack."

We'd only successfully pulled off such an attack on a couple of occasions; usually our stifled laughter under his bed in anticipation of his arrival would give us away the minute Jim walked up the stairs. But on the rare occasion when we were successful, the hysterical delight that followed was worth more than I can describe. We would spend the next week recounting it dozens of times to anyone who would listen, and with each retelling, Jim's fright got more and more exaggerated.

Something about this early childhood memory led me to sneak up on Leslie early in our marriage. I wasn't doing it to be mean. The little boy within me just had a spontaneous thought that was too good to pass up. As Leslie was rummaging around in a closet in the upper loft of our city apartment, I simply snuck into it without her notice. I barely breathed as I waited. Minutes later, she discovered my head resting on a box she was getting ready to move. I didn't say a word. I didn't holler. I didn't have to. Leslie did enough hollering on her own.

She literally jumped back as I quickly moved out from behind the boxes. "I'm so sorry, are you okay?" I asked as I put my arms around her. We both fell to the floor, and Leslie, recovering from her fright, started to laugh. "All I saw was your head," she said. "How long were you in there?" As we literally rolled on the floor laughing, Leslie pinned my shoulders down and said, "Tonight—while you sleep, pal."

> To really know someone is to have loved and hated him in turn.
> *Marcel Jouhandeau*

I don't know that Leslie ever really got even with me for that sneak attack, but I do know that our marriage has suffered from other sneaky things that have crept into our relationship and scared us both. And chances are the same has happened to your marriage, too.

Have you ever wondered to yourself, *If this marriage is supposed to be so good, why do I sometimes feel so bad?* If so, your marriage has probably been the victim of one of several predictable sneak attacks on the modern marriage. In this chapter, we expose a half dozen of the most common and subtle saboteurs of today's marriage. These are things that slowly sneak into our relationship without so much as a whisper. They are busyness, irritation, boredom, drift, debt, and pain.

Busyness

So much of marriage is consumed with "doing life"—with each of us busily checking off items on unromantic lists that keep reappearing in different forms. So our "quality time" ends up being in front of the TV while eating our dinner and reading the mail. Why are our schedules so packed? Most of us point to work. We now have nearly 40 million two-income couples in America. Nearly a third of us take work home at least once each week, and more than 70 percent of us do work-related tasks during the weekend. A recent five-year study, not surprisingly, found work (especially the work we bring home) to blame for the bulk of the stress we experience at home.[1]

Why do we work so much? Dr. George Wald, a Harvard biologist who won the Nobel Prize, may have the answer: "What one really needs is not Nobel laureates but love. How do you think one gets to be a Nobel laureate? Wanting love, that's how. Wanting it so bad one works all the time and ends up a Nobel laureate. It's a consolation prize. What matters is love."[2]

Regardless of the reasons, most husbands and wives agree that they are too busy. The good news for all of us in this camp is that we can change. In fact, of all the problems that quietly sneak up on good marriages, busyness is one that can be changed most easily.

The solution is found in stripping away nonessential and "urgent" demands on our time until our schedules reflect the value of our marriage. Marriage rarely seems urgent, so it ends up low on our priority list. Lest you think that rearranging your priorities is the only part of this solution to overactivity, let us quickly warn you that fewer work hours doesn't automatically solve the problem. Why? Because what we *say* about our priorities doesn't always match what we *do*.

> Things which matter most must never be at the mercy of things which matter least.
>
> *Goethe*

A recent poll indicates a good marriage and family life is how most people say they measure success. Eight of ten people say they admire someone who puts family before work; nearly half say they've changed jobs to have more family time. But research has shown that in spite of these expressed values, people's working hours continue to rise, while time together at home falls.[3] The message is clear. We must not only prune our activities in order to have time together, we must then spend that time constructively *together*, not surfing the Internet alone or reading a book in isolation. For many successful couples, this means developing a hobby together, not merely intending to make time for a hobby that you never get to.

Real-Life Problem Solvers

How We Tamed the Busyness Monster

Steve and Thanne Moore
Married in 1981

With our two kids in tow, we moved our family from Texas to Seattle during our seventh year of marriage. While Steve jumped into his new job full throttle, I was busy moving us into a temporary living arrangement and hunting for a new house. It was a quick start to a new phase of life that only got more fast-paced. Not so very long after our arrival in town, we had a third arrival ourselves. We now had two kids in school and a baby. Our days were relentless. Little League. Car pools. Music lessons. Board meetings. Business trips. Late nights. Early mornings. Oh, yes, and a marriage too. We expected the pace of life to eventually slow down, but it didn't. Though we weren't about to admit it, the problem was chronic. The speed of our shared life was hurtling out of control. We were moving faster and doing more than two married people should ever even consider. Busy? That's an understatement!

Steve's Experience

We had been going at a pretty hectic pace for some time, and I was more focused on how to survive it than manage it. Whenever Thanne complained about our frantic pace, I would usually tell her to lighten up and take a rest. I assured her we wouldn't be this busy forever. As you might guess, my sermonettes were never appreciated. Looking back, I must confess that I was putting pressure on Thanne to keep up while I was running an unrealistic sprint.

Thanne's Experience

I knew Steve had a lot of pressures at work. His days were jam-packed. And I didn't want to burden him with more pressures at home. He was always willing to help when I asked, but I didn't want to have to ask. I wanted him to pick it up intuitively. From my perspective, the "crash and burn" of the moment was just the symptom of the larger problem of deciding how we would tackle the busyness monster that had invaded our marriage.

How We Solved the Problem

We came up with several strategies that have helped us manage our time-starved lives. First, we both agreed that we needed a regular time that was just for us, a weekly time when we could kick back, enjoy one another's company, and get away from the hurried pace. This became a time not to problem-solve about work or plan our budget. This was a time for fun. The second thing we did was get ahead of the busyness curve by planning our calendar three or four weeks in advance. This brought more coordination to our schedules and created fewer pressure-cooker surprises. It also helped us schedule family time first, instead of squeezing it in after the schedule was already full. Third, we planned big events we could look forward to every few months, something that would be a total break in our routine. This might be a road trip to Montana or camping in a local state park. Finally, we make our schedules and our busy pace a matter of ongoing prayer. Busyness is not a problem to be solved one time and never faced again. It is an ongoing challenge.

A Word to Other Couples

Commit yourselves to battling the busyness monster by building in breaks that allow your souls to catch up.

Exercise 12: Taking Control of Your Time-Starved Marriage

Stephen R. Covey, the undisputed champion of personal management, is known for teaching individuals to identify their priorities and structure their lives accordingly. He uses the analogy of directing one's life by a compass rather than a clock. Those individuals who live out their priorities continually check their compass to be sure they are headed in the direction they desire. Every couple whose relationship has been quietly ensnared by busyness can do well to think in these same terms. This workbook exercise will help you do that.

Irritability

Let's admit it. The breakneck speed of most days, the busyness we just talked about, leads to a character flaw most of us would rather not acknowledge. If we are busy and stressed, we've probably become cranky and grouchy with our partner. We didn't start out this way, of course. When we first married, we were the epitome of kindness and sensitivity. But somewhere along the line, without any effort on our part, a side of us was revealed that had become surprisingly testy, touchy, and downright irritable.

Have you ever blurted out driving instructions from the passenger seat, even though you knew that would chill an otherwise enjoyable date with your spouse? Have you ever snapped an order at your mate and then tagged a gratuitous "please" on the end that was clearly an afterthought? Have you ever grumbled and groused over having to plan yet another family meal when you used to take pride in your culinary efforts?

Most of us justify our irritability with thoughts such as, *This isn't really me treating my soul mate poorly; I'm really a caring person. This is just me after a particularly grueling day. The real me will show up later.* We convince ourselves that our grouchiness is a temporary condition that will go away as soon as we pay the bills, throw our friend's baby shower, or complete an important project at work. But over time, we realize our rationale is wearing thin. We gradually learn we can't even convince ourselves, let alone our spouse. So what can a grump do? Plenty.

It begins—and ends—with paying special attention to how we treat our partner. Can you imagine if your home was bugged? For the last forty-eight hours every conversation and every comment you made to your spouse was on tape. Feeling queasy? Even worse, you are now going to have to sit down and listen to yourself and how you spoke to your partner over this time period. It's a frightening thought for most of us. And it's probably a good thing we

> To do the same thing over and over again is not only boredom: it is to be controlled by rather than to control what you do.
>
> *Heraclitus*

won't have to endure it. But to change our grouchy ways, we will need some method of monitoring our interactions. Why? Because awareness is often curative. Simply recognizing what you are doing, when you are doing it, and how it makes your spouse feel, is enough to get you moving out of your grouchy plight.

Work on increasing your awareness by keeping a journal for a week or more to record the kinds of things you say. You may discover, for example, that you are particularly irritable at certain times of the day, or when you are hungry. These are important things to know. If you're feeling particularly brave, you may want to invite your partner to give you feedback on how he or she felt at various points during the day as a result of your interactions. However you go about it, raising awareness of your ways will become the key to keeping your irritability under control.

Boredom

"There are nights when we sit by the dinner table with nothing to say to each other," a client recently told us, "and I remember all the nights in restaurants when I have watched such silence between other couples with smug contempt, wondering how they ever got that way."

The pain in this woman's voice was piercing. She wasn't describing a marriage that was marred by crisis. There were no angry yelling matches in this home, no real fights at all to speak of. She was suffering from a lifeless boredom that had settled over her marriage like a thick fog that kept growing thicker. "I'm so tired of the humdrum routine of this relationship," she complained, "I'm afraid I'm going to do something I'll regret." She went on to describe a situation with a man she knew from work. "I've never had an affair and I don't want one now, but the thought does pass through my mind."

We weren't surprised. For the spouse who feels trapped in a boring marriage, an affair seems like his or her road to excitement. Thankfully, this woman had enough self-discipline to pass up the excitement that was guaranteed to wreak carnage on her husband and children. Instead, she opted to work with her spouse to bring their marriage back from the brink of devastating boredom.

Boredom is one of the most silent of all marital saboteurs. It sneaks up so quietly that usually only one of the partners knows it has arrived. In the case we just described, the husband was completely oblivious to his wife's feelings until she disclosed them. He was simply walking through the motions of his daily existence: working, eating, sleeping. Oh, he knew the passion level of his marriage had dropped off, the vitality and enthusiasm had dissipated. He just thought that's what eventually happens in a marriage flanked with work and child-care demands. And he was right, to some degree. Every marriage goes through periodic doldrums. Isolated low points don't pose a major threat, but chronic boredom can be fatal.

The problem of boredom is so pervasive in relationships that you can pick up almost any popular women's magazine to find dozens of suggestions for "spicing up your marriage." They will tell you to get out of your rut by doing new things: buy satin sheets, play the latest CDs, make homemade ice cream in the dead of winter, rearrange your furniture, and so on. We're not knocking any of these creative suggestions, but the real secret to transcending boredom in marriage has little to do with these remedies. When you take a good look at why you are bored, you will find that your boredom stems from a condition that has put the most interesting and exciting parts of your partner to sleep. It's nobody's fault, necessarily, but the result is that you find your partner, and thus your marriage, one-dimensional.

> Stirring the oatmeal is a humble act . . . it represents a willingness to find meaning in the simple unromantic tasks: earning a living, living within a budget, putting out the garbage.
>
> Robert A. Johnson

So what's the answer? You need to reawaken the sleeping parts of your partner. If she used to love reading poetry, pick up a copy of T. S. Eliot and read it yourself. If you'd never taken much of an interest in poetry before, it's no wonder that she allowed her interest in it to lie dormant.

If your husband used to love tennis and hasn't played in years, buy a couple of new rackets. Or maybe he loved collecting baseball cards as a kid and hasn't talked about his collection for eons. You could attend a show for collectors with him.

If you are bored in your marriage, it's because there are interests and energies your partner has that aren't being expressed. It's your job to bring them back to life and then enjoy them with him or her. This will require some stretching on your part, but the new vigor it will give your relationship is well worth it.

You need not resign yourself to a boring marriage. So quit yawning and rediscover your spouse. When you break through the boredom barrier that has beset your relationship, you'll discover you are capable of far more than you thought. You'll begin to enjoy a vitality in your marriage that you never knew was there.

Real-Life Problem Solvers

How We Brought Back the Fun in Our Marriage

Neil and Marylyn Warren
Married in 1959

We entered a rut early in our marriage. All the fun seemed to seep right through the cracks in the floor of our relationship. We thought it was a phase, something that would soon pass, but it lasted far too long. When Neil entered the University of Chicago to earn his Ph.D., he buried himself in his studies. Our three daughters were all born during this time, and on all three of their birth certificates, "Father's Occupation" was listed as "student."

That's okay, we'd say to ourselves. *Once we get through school, things will be different.* So when we finally graduated and Neil landed a job in California as a professor, we were ready for a change. We were ready for romance. We were ready for fun. After all our delayed gratification, we moved that summer, set up our new life—but instead of shifting gears, we fell right back into the same routine.

Neil's Experience

With a new academic job and new pressures to produce, I had no time for celebrating. My first course was on the philosopher Schleiermacher. I couldn't even spell Schleiermacher, let alone wax eloquent about him. Another graduate course I taught was on statistics, and virtually every student in the class was a mathematical genius who knew more about math than I did. I worked my tail off, night and day, including weekends. I was scared to death that, after all my education, I would make a fool of myself and prove inadequate to the expectations of these students, as well as my family. This was an anxiety hurricane for me. I was intent on surviving and never meant to put our marriage on hold.

Marylyn's Experience

All through graduate school, I hung onto the hope that we would enter our own utopia as soon as the Ph.D. was secured. The sacrificing would be in the past, and we would live the life we wanted. I didn't understand Neil's continuing obsession with work. It was a lonely time for both of us. I needed his support, and I'm sure he needed mine. But the pressure-packed years had sapped our marital spontaneity. At the end of a twelve-hour day, Neil would come home used up. Just like our grad school days, he had no interest in or energy for communication. We were still in our rut, and I was at my wit's end.

How We Solved the Problem

I (Marylyn) decided I wasn't about to let our marriage be undone by the mundane. And I wasn't willing to settle for a mediocre marriage, either. The first step to solving our problem came when I spoke up. In the past, I'd sometimes swallow my pain, but I didn't do that this time. I spoke up loud and clear, and Neil listened.

I (Neil) agreed that something had to be done, starting with our channels of communication. For the first time in our marriage, I really talked. I told her about work, about my hopes, about my fears. And Marylyn did the same. We discovered together just how much marital communication reduces loneliness, how much vitality it adds to our relationship.

Our turnabout didn't end there. We set aside money for baby-sitters and started dating again. We spent our evenings together, and in the mornings we started talking about everything the day would hold. I (Neil) set aside work and planned surprise trips to celebrate our important dates. We got into a small group with three other couples to meet every other week, and Marylyn came by my school for lunch every so often.

As a result, we literally climbed out of our rut and put the fun back in our relationship. We became each other's dearest and most trusted friend—and we're still having a blast!

A Word to Other Couples

When your marriage falls into a rut or becomes mundane, remember why you fell in love in the first place; relish the romance and fun of your friendship.

Drift

In a previous chapter we mentioned that many couples complain, and even quit marriage, because they have "drifted apart." Over the years they have lost touch with each other, and their connection is not as strong because their interests have diverged. Their union is not breaking because of a single, cataclysmic event. It has eroded gradually in small, barely discernible ways. After a matter of years they wake up and wonder, *Who is this person I married?*

Does this sound familiar? Let us ask a few more questions. Do you find yourself looking for alternatives to being with your spouse? Do you depend less and less on your partner? Have you quit sharing the details of your life with him or her? Has your sexual interest waned? If you are answering yes to these questions, it's time to get vigilant.

You can begin by reordering your priorities. Time demands are always barriers to oneness, but when your marriage slips to a lower rung, the time demands multiply. If your work, your church, or even your children's needs are taking precedence over your relationship with your spouse, it's time to set a new standard and put your marriage at the top of your list.

Second, you need to make specific requests of your mate for help in some area, even if you don't need help. It could be grocery shopping or yard work. The goal is to work on something together.

Third, you can reverse your drift rate by sharing more information about the daily routine of your life with your spouse, even mundane experiences.

Finally, we strongly urge you to save your money and schedule a special weekend away at a hotel, maybe a place

> Marriage must constantly fight against a monster which devours everything: routine.
>
> *Honore De Balzac*

you enjoyed together earlier in your marriage. Do this within the next few weeks. Don't wait. And if you can afford it, schedule another getaway for a month or two later—if not an overnight getaway, try an all-day outing. If this suggestion sounds like a cliché or something you've heard before, it's because every marriage expert knows the potential of such a weekend experience for the couple who has drifted apart. So don't allow more time to come between you; begin making your plans today.

Most couples who drift apart still care deeply for one another. The only problem is that they now feel so different. You don't have to allow the increasing gap between you and your partner to grow any wider. You have the power to pull it together and enjoy meaningful connections with your partner in areas of your life you may have thought your partner would never share.

Exercise 13: Getting to Know You . . . All Over Again

Every marriage is at risk for drift. If you have experienced a drift from your partner, be it big or small, you probably have lost track of the person you once knew so well. Perhaps the intimacies you once knew about each other have seemingly evaporated. If this rings true for you, take some time to do this workbook exercise. It will help you reconnect with your spouse.

Debt

In a time when the expected American norm is two shiny cars, a new house, and designer clothes, couples are more in debt than ever before. And each year, many marriages dig themselves deeper into debt, until it eventually dawns on them that they may not be able to get out. The debt we're talking about is not your mortgage or even your car payment. If you are feeling the financial squeeze of what Ron Blue calls the "Borrower Constrictor," you probably owe major money on your credit cards. The average American carries a credit card balance of about $6,000, on which he or she pays 18 percent interest or more. This means that the average person has a cash outlay of almost $1,000 per year in credit card interest charges alone.[4]

Here's our fear. Instead of taking these startling statistics as a wake-up call, you may be taking a perverse comfort in the fact that you are not alone, that other couples are just as financially strung out as you. It may be true. But we can assure you that you do not have to live that way. If your marriage is feeling the strain of trying to carry increasing accumulations of debt, you can begin lightening your load starting today.

The first step in getting out of debt is to recognize how much money you owe. Once you have a specific figure, a grand total of the debt you now have, you have two avenues toward reducing it. You can increase your income, or you can reduce your expenses. For most people, it's easier to do the latter. So the next step is finding where you can cut your spending. We learned a valuable lesson early on in our marriage when we discovered that by simply not using credit cards we spent less. In fact, one study has shown that people who pay for their groceries with a credit card spend up to 54 percent more.[5] Why? Most experts say that when we pay with a credit card, we don't register the pain of actually letting go of cash. Whether it be fewer times eating out, buying clothes at bargain stores, or simply putting an end to impulse purchases, you must find specific ways to spend less. If you spent just $3 less each day, you would save more than $1,000 in a year. So don't convince yourself that small sacrifices make no difference.

> Marriage halves our griefs,
> doubles our joys,
> and quadruples our expenses.
> *English proverb*

We have one more suggestion for getting out of debt. It is to become accountable to someone. This can be embarrassing if you are in a great deal of debt, but it is all the more essential. To stay on track with your repayment plan, it is crucial to have someone you both respect who will keep your feet to the fire.

Getting out of debt will be one of the most rewarding things you'll ever do as a couple. Not only will you celebrate a concrete accomplishment, you'll tear down an invisible barrier that has interfered with your intimacy for far too long.

Real-Life Problem Solvers

How We Survived Financial Debt

Doug and Jana McKinley
Married in 1985

We were happily married for six years and living in Ft. Wayne, Indiana, when we had the opportunity to start a business in Chicago with a friend. Until the business could fund itself, arrangements were made for us to receive a base salary for the first year or two—"guaranteed." In no time at all, we sold our home in Ft. Wayne, moved our family to Chicago, and dove headfirst into a new business. But what we thought was an exciting adventure proved to be the toughest challenge of our married life. Unbeknownst to us, there turned out to be no financial backing in place to start Doug's new business. We were now in a new state, a new home, and raising a new baby, with no foreseeable way to financially support any of us.

Doug's Experience

I was excited about the opportunity to start a business with a friend, and I naively trusted him to help it work out. When it didn't, I was in a state of pure panic. I was hurt by my friend and blamed everything possible. But after all the anger and all the blame, I still had no job. The kind of work I was trained to do would require months of building networks and referrals. I protected myself by ignoring the whole issue, not realizing how much stress was building in my marriage. I kicked into provider mode. I channeled all of my energies into finding creative ways to generate income.

Jana's Experience

After the initial shock and disbelief wore off, I carried anger around for quite a while. I nursed anger at the friend who had promised the money and anger at myself for not seeing this unfold and putting a stop to it. I recall being more upset at myself than Doug, because it was more in my nature than his to be cautious and ask questions. I felt stuck and betrayed. While Doug did what he could to make money, I concentrated on taking care of our baby boy. We were surviving in our own separate worlds. Because of the financial strain, it took time to put the emotional pieces of our marriage back together.

How We Solved the Problem

We were forced to devise a financial plan that included a meager budget until Doug could find a stable job and we could get back on our feet. It was a matter of survival. To help us meet our immediate financial needs, I (Doug) turned to my father-in-law for a loan. It was the most humbling experience of my life. He was compassionate and gentle with us as we confessed our major financial blunder. Next, we sold both our cars to get out from under the loan payments. A friend allowed us to use his car until we were able to afford one later on. We continually acknowledged God's faithfulness to us throughout this process. Never have we been more dependent on him and other people—as well as each other. Ultimately, we asked forgiveness of each other and learned to communicate more effectively. Now, when we are faced with a new decision, we pray about it, gather information and wisdom from others that will help us make a sound decision, and wait to proceed until we feel strongly led one way or another.

A Word to Other Couples

Continually communicate with each other about decisions that will impact your finances. Seek guidance from those in the know, ask every question you can think of, and put your financial plans in writing.

Pain from the Past

Sadly, one of the worst things to sneak up on a good marriage is pain from the past. We have friends who were married nearly twenty years before she disclosed to him a secret she thought she'd never tell a soul. As a little girl, she had been sexually molested by a neighbor for more than three years. She kept it a secret for decades because she was embarrassed and ashamed. Her husband never considered that his wife had quietly endured such suffering, not until she broke down uncontrollably on a trip they made together to visit her childhood home. Since that time, they've been working together to heal her damaged emotions.

We know another couple whose marriage bumped into a painful past when the husband slowly realized how his early relationship with his alcoholic father was interfering with his marriage years later. He'd learned as a child not to show his feelings, especially affection. His father ridiculed him for such things. As an adult, just a few years into his marriage, he continued to hear his father's voice echoing in his mind each time he tried to express his love for his wife and kids.

Many of us have wounds and scars we've carried into our marriage, painful pasts that had nothing to do with our partner. But sooner or later they impact our marriage just the same. The emotions may have been buried, but they are still alive and lurking below the surface. One of the most common painful pasts we bring into a marriage is a deep sense of unworthiness, a continual feeling of inadequacy and inferiority. It's often the result of a child who reaches out for love and approval but instead got the opposite and now carries the pain of rejection as an adult. Such pain cannot help but to sneak up on an unsuspecting spouse and disturb a good marriage.

One group of researchers who has studied the link between early childhood pain and the social bonds of adulthood concluded that "those most in need of the support provided by a good marriage may not be able to benefit from it because the ability to form close relationships may itself be impaired by earlier adversity."[6] The researchers found that spouses who had a negative bonding experience with parents often have difficulty or may even avoid getting intimate in their marriage for fear of failure or rejection.

Exercise 14: Healing Your Painful Past

If you have pain from your past that is hurting your marriage in the present, the road to recovery requires healing, for you and maybe your relationship too. This workbook exercise is designed to facilitate the beginning stages of that healing by having you take a closer look at just how your past may be impacting your marriage. This exercise requires honest reflection, compassion from your partner, and time. Plenty of time—both now and later.

In all honesty, we can't begin to do justice to the steps you will need to take in this direction; there are too many personal variables. We strongly encourage you to seek the help of a competent counselor who can walk you through a healing journey that may require only a few sessions. We will have more to say about this in the next chapter. But be assured, God has provided a means to help you transcend the pain from your past. It does not have to interfere with your present. In fact, the marriage you cherish may be the means of grace God will use to restore your spirit.

For Reflection

1. Has busyness crept into your marriage? Are you feeling like your schedules have collided with romance and other things you enjoy about being a couple? What is something you can do this week to keep busyness from interfering with your love life?
2. Irritation is something few of us like to own up to, but if you find that this "temporary" trait has stayed too long, try to identify specific times when it is most apparent. What are they? How can these moments in your marriage be handled to minimize the irritation?
3. Consider, by name, each of the unhelpful ruts your marriage is in. How did they occur? What is keeping you from getting out of these ruts to create some new excitement in your marriage?
4. Of the half-dozen bad things that sneak up on good marriages—busyness, irritation, boredom, drift, debt, and pain—which one would you identify as your most damaging? What have you tried in the past to combat it, and what can you do today that will make it better?

Many an inherited sorrow that has marred
a life has been breathed into no human ear.
George Eliot

---

how to solve any problem in five (not-so-easy) steps

Discover the "slumbering powers" of your marriage
and use this proven plan for revolutionizing your love life.

Deep within humans dwell those slumbering powers;
powers that would astonish them,
that they never dreamed of possessing;
forces that would revolutionize their lives
if aroused and put into action.

Orison Marden

If you were to get out a yellow pad of paper and outline ways to make a marriage miserable, I doubt you could come up with a strategy that tops the real-life relationship of Ted and Liz. They sailed along smoothly in the early years of marriage, working through common struggles such as communication breakdowns. But shortly after the birth of their first child, Ted and Liz were bowled over by a series of unpredictable hits. First, Liz was struck by breast cancer. It was an anguishing experience that impacted every aspect of her life and her marriage. Four years later, Ted lost his job because of an affair with a woman at work. Repentant, he begged Liz to stay with him, and, after much agonizing, she did. But as they worked to repair the immediate damage Ted inflicted on their relationship, it was compounded by his lack of work. Picking up the pieces of his life made seeking out a job all the more difficult, and the couple soon fell into financial straits. Their difficulties did not end there. Ted's younger brother was killed in an automobile accident, and that pushed Ted over the edge. He sank into a severe clinical depression, leaving Liz with a small baby, a meager budget, and an emotionally detached husband.

Some—maybe most—couples would not recover from all these calamities. Any single one of them is enough to bring down many a very good marriage. But today, nearly two decades after the birth of their first child, Ted and Liz are still very much together and happily married. If you didn't know their story, you'd probably have no idea of the suffering they've endured. Why? Because they learned to battle their bad things. Not quickly. Not easily. But over time, gradually, step by step, Ted and Liz refurbished their marriage. And if you were to get out your yellow pad of paper and outline just what a happy couple looks like, you'd be hard pressed to find another couple that would come closer to that description today than Ted and Liz.

What Good Couples Do Right

Marriages that have bumped into problems do not recover quickly. Not generally, anyway. And smart couples do not buy into instant success plans that promise hurried ways to heal hearts or rapid roads to renewed relationships. They know better and, instead, expect slow progress, steadily building one marriage accomplishment upon another, like a game that is won one play at a time, or a building that is built brick by brick. Smart couples don't expect the world to fall into their laps. It never has. But somewhere deep in the soul of every marriage, a husband and wife will find what Orison Marden calls their "slumbering powers." And these astonishing powers, when awoken, will rise up, look bad fortune in the face, and begin to revolutionize their relationship. It may be a gradual revolution, but it is a trust-building, heart-healing, love-renewing revolution, just the same.

We know you may be weary. You may be dog tired of trying. You've imagined the distance your relationship has to travel, the hills you have to climb, and you wonder if it is even possible. But it is. Remember the words of Dag Hammarskjold, secretary-general of the United Nations, when he said, "Never measure the height of a mountain, until you have reached the top. Then you will see how low it was."

> Goodness is the only investment that never fails.
>
> *Henry David Thoreau*

Every revolution begins with a battle. And in the case of marriage, it is a battle against the bad things that have had the audacity to attack love. But no bad thing can stand the wrath of a husband and wife who decide to marshal their might against it. Once the dormant powers of a couple's love have kicked in, an extraordinary force emerges that will not stand idly by while their marriage gets kicked about. *We won't settle for a mediocre marriage,* these ardent couples shout. Or, *We won't let this thing beat us. We will survive.* And they do. They find the strength to make the journey, to climb the mountains, to battle their calamities. These are not uncommon couples blessed with abilities beyond reach. These are husbands and wives like you and like me.

In this chapter we equip you with the five best tools every good marriage uses to battle bad things. They are . . .

Ownership—taking responsibility for the good as well as the bad

Hope—believing that good wins over bad

Empathy—walking in your partner's shoes

Forgiveness—healing the hurts you don't deserve

Commitment—living the love you promised

This list is a tall order for mere mortals, but it is within reach. And with God's help, you can find the power you never dreamed of possessing to bring each of these qualities to life in your marriage.

Ownership—Taking Responsibility for the Good and the Bad

Couples in counseling almost always believe their problems rest mainly with the other person. Like gun slingers from the Old West, they draw their dueling fingers and point to each other's flaws and foibles. They say things such as, *If it weren't for your anger, we might have a real marriage. If you didn't lie about so many things, maybe I could trust you. If you were ever interested in having a conversation, I might be interested in having sex.*

> All adversity is really an opportunity for our souls to grow.
>
> *John Gray*

Every competent counselor knows that no matter what the marriage problem, the system that sustains it is found in both people. Like a mobile hanging from the ceiling, a change to one piece impacts the equilibrium of the entire structure. In the same way, every marriage maintains balance as two people shift their positions, their attitudes, and their behaviors to counter one another. Thus in a long-term relationship, complete responsibility for problems rarely rests entirely on the shoulders of one person. Before a single step is taken, before a move is made, spouses will need to realize that it's not *who's* wrong, but *what's* wrong that counts.

When Bill McCartney founded Promise Keepers in 1990, the ministry dedicated to building men of integrity, he truly believed that his marriage to Lyndi was fine. His commitment to both coaching another stellar season at the University of Colorado as well as building up this new ministry, however, provided the perfect camouflage for hypocrisy in his personal life. "It may sound unbelievable," he writes in his book *Sold Out*, "but while Promise Keepers was spiritually inspiring to my core, my hard-charging approach to the ministry was distracting me from being, in the truest sense, a promise keeper to my own family."

McCartney points to two events that showed him he was out of touch and avoiding responsibility for the condition of his own marriage. One was a Promise Keepers rally where men were told to write down the number their wives would give their marriages if rating them on a scale of one to ten. He had to admit with embarrassment to the other men on the platform that Lyndi would probably give their marriage only a six.

Then in the fall of 1994, McCartney heard a speaker make this pointed statement: "If you want to know about a man's character, then look into the face of his wife. Whatever he has invested in or withheld from her will be reflected in her countenance." Something clicked in McCartney. As he puts it, he escorted his "wounded wife" out of the parking lot, determined that rebuilding his marriage would require him to take drastic measures. Shortly thereafter, Coach McCartney announced his retirement from the University of Colorado in order to spend time with Lyndi. To do so, he gave up the ten years remaining on his $350,000-a-year contract.

Sports Illustrated called it "un-American." McCartney called it taking responsibility for the state of his marriage.

> Good timber does not grow with ease; the stronger the wind, the stronger the trees.
>
> *J. Willard Marriott*

The single best day in every marriage is when two partners take responsibility for their part of the pie. This doesn't require anything as dramatic as quitting one's job, but it can be just as scary. Taking ownership for anything of significance presents new fears. This must be what Nelson Mandela was thinking when he said, "Our greatest fear is not that we will discover that we are inadequate, but that we will discover that we are powerful beyond measure."

In the short run, it is far easier to avoid responsibility for our problems by blaming someone else. But in the long haul, admitting mistakes and owning up to our part of the problem is the single most powerful predictor of turning something bad into something good.

Exercise 15: Owning Up

"There can be no true response without responsibility, and there can be no responsibility without response," according to theologian Arthur Vogel. Do you agree? His point is that you cannot separate responsibility from actions. In this workbook exercise we help you not only clarify the responsibility quotient in your marriage, we help you bring about the actions to improve it.

Hope—By Believing That Good Wins over Bad

Once a husband and wife, together, take responsibility for the good as well as the bad in their relationship, a small seedling of hope is planted. Its tiny roots are found in a rich soil, free from negative thinking about what somebody should have done or what somebody didn't do. It is a seedling that, in time, will sprout optimism.

I (Les) learned the powerful potential of hope while I was working as a medical psychologist on the burn unit at the University of Washington School of Medicine. As part of a two-year study examining how patient attitudes might impact their recovery, it was found that those patients who described themselves as hopeful recovered far more quickly and effectively than those who didn't. One hardly needs a study, of course, to know the value of hope to the human spirit.

But when it comes to a marriage burned by something bad, some of us need a little more convincing. After all, hope is a risk, and we fear that what we hope for may not happen.

We once asked a group of students at our university if they had hope. Most of them, as best we can remember, said they did. But one student raised his hand and asked an intriguing question: "How would I know if I have hope?" What he was wondering was what the experience of hope looks like. What are its ingredients? I don't know that we gave him a satisfactory answer that day, but we have since concluded that the inward experience of hope involves at least three things.[1]

First, hope includes *desire*. We want a kind of marriage we do not yet have. Hope also includes *belief*. We believe that the kind of marriage we want is possible. But hope may also include *worry*. Though it is entirely possible to have the kind of marriage we want, we are not completely convinced that we will ever have it. We fear the possibility that it may not happen, and the greater our fear, the less hope we have. That's why human hope is always a risk.

> Thee lift me and I'll lift thee, and we will ascend together.
>
> *Quaker proverb*

If you are having difficulty churning up hope for your marriage, take comfort in knowing that you have more hope than you think. It may not be readily accessible; your worry and fear may be keeping it hidden. But you do have hope. "Hope is bred in the bone," as our late friend Lew Smedes put it. "Our spirits were made for hope the way our hearts were made to love and our brains were made to think."[2] A "life instinct" is what Karl Menninger called hope.[3] The ancient story of Pandora and her box reveals that all people have always known in their hearts that they could not live without hope.

Pandora's mythical story begins when the Greek god Zeus came down from Mt. Olympus and gave her a treasure chest crammed with everything a man and woman would need to live happily forever. The chest was sealed, and Zeus sternly warned Pandora not to open it. But her curiosity got the better of her, and she pried open the lid to steal a look. All the blessings flew out of the chest and scattered themselves just out of man's reach. One blessing stayed in the chest, however, for both man and woman to keep. It was hope. And as long as hope is kept alive, we have the strength to keep striving for the blessings that have flown beyond our reach.

Hope keeps love alive. Stop hoping and marriage dies. As long as we imagine a better marriage and keep believing we will one day enjoy it, the battle against bad things can still be won. Hope lets us see that our world just might be set straight on its hinges once more.

Exercise 16: High Hopes—Even When You're Hurting

Hope can sometimes seem like a rare and fragile plant that needs careful cultivation. And most days in most marriages, there is barely enough time to take care of the rudimentaries of life, let alone the more delicate aspects of our relationship. This workbook exercise will help you cultivate the flowering aspects of hope in your marriage. No matter how small your hope may currently seem, this exercise will help you grow it.

Empathy—By Walking in Your Partner's Shoes

"Before you leave this auditorium, we want you to pick up a small box you'll find on a table in the foyer. Open it once you get home and let its contents run loose. It's a box of empathy."

We've often dreamed of being able to say something like this to a group of couples who have come to one of our marriage seminars. We don't know of another quality that can do more for a marriage than empathy—that capacity to put yourself in your partner's shoes and see the world from his or her perspective; to imagine what life must be like to be lived in his or her skin. It's what poet Walt Whitman was getting at back in 1855 when he wrote his masterwork, *Leaves of Grass*: "I do not ask how the wounded one feels; I, myself, *become* the wounded one."

Research has shown that 90 percent of our struggles in marriage would be resolved if we did nothing more than see that problem from our partner's perspective. Empathy is the heart of love. Yet loving couples neglect it to their peril. Why? Because it's tough to do. Empathy calls for loving our partner with both our head and heart, concurrently. Most of us do one or the other pretty well; we either feel our partner's pain with our heart, or we try to solve their problem with our head. To do both can be tricky. But that is the charge and the gift of empathy.

> Hope has two beautiful daughters. Their names are anger and courage; anger at the way things are, and courage to see that they do not remain the way they are.
>
> St. Augustine

Are some people unable to empathize? Only narcissists and deviants with no conscience. Everyone else can use their head and heart to put themselves in their partner's shoes. It's been proven. Like hope, we have something in our nature, right from the beginning, that provides the makings for human empathy. When a content newborn baby hears another baby crying, for example, it also begins to wail. It's not just the loud noise, but the sound of a fellow human in distress that triggers the baby's crying, research finds.[4]

So if it has been a while since you worked on empathy in your marriage, allow us to make a suggestion. No matter what your particular struggles may be, no matter what bad things your marriage has bumped into, we are convinced you can soon see the benefits of empathy by conducting a small exercise together. It has to do with understanding the home your partner grew up in.

Most people don't realize the extent to which the marriage they create is a product of the marriage they observed growing up. For better or worse, every husband and wife brings behaviors, beliefs, quirks, and roles into their marriage that they are not even aware of. Like an actor in a dramatic performance following a script (the one we observed growing up), each of us plays a part in our marriage to which we normally haven't given much thought. As a result, we become entangled in a story about us that we never intended to write. Why? Because we've never taken the time to really explore each other's early family environments. Without knowing it, we absorbed ways of being a wife or a husband from our family of origin—and we formed standards for our spouse to live up to in his or her role too. That's why some good couples have a difficult marriage.

Would it make any difference if you could go back in time and observe firsthand the kind of home and the experiences your spouse had as a child? Would the role he or she plays today as your mate make more sense? Almost certainly. It did for former pro-football player with the Minnesota Vikings Doug Kingsriter. He writes about a time when he and his wife, Debbie, got stranded at her parents' home for three days because of an ice storm. With plenty of time to kill, Doug ended up watching all of Debbie's home movies her family had made over the years. He watched how her family celebrated her birthdays and how she worked to be Miss Teenage America. He saw how her parents interacted, the models of marriage they provided Debbie. "I literally watched her grow up," Doug said. "By the third day, I realized the girl in the films was the same person I'd married ...

> A man, to be greatly good,
> must imagine intensely
> and comprehensively;
> he must put himself
> in the place of another.
> *Percy B. Shelley*

it allowed me to really see Debbie for the first time." He called it a "moment of awakening" in his marriage. "From then on, I listened much more closely to Debbie ... I treated her with more respect."[5]

You may not have home movies to watch, but you can explore the past with your partner just the same as you try to imagine what it would have been like to grow up in his or her shoes.

> A good marriage is the union of two forgivers.
> *Ruth Bell Graham*

Rita, an only child, grew up in a home where she felt cherished by a mom and dad who went out of their way to care for her. They were continually looking after Rita and each other. So when Rita married Vince, the middle child in a family with several siblings, she made the erroneous assumption so many people make in marriage, that "what's good for me is good for you." She cared for him the way she wanted to be cared for. She brought him snacks, for example, whether he was hungry or not. She saw this as an act of kindness. He saw it as a waste of food. She would set out a clean shirt for him to wear in the morning. She saw this as being thoughtful. He saw it as being smothered. It was all too much for Vince. So much "caring" became downright irritating to him. Rita had no idea why he was so often annoyed. Rita thought she was helping when, in truth, she was only making matters worse. It was nothing personal. Vince simply felt smothered by too much caring. The point? Rita will never succeed in loving Vince until she first puts herself in his shoes. The same is true, by the way, for Vince.

When we empathize with our partner, we will never look at him or her the same way again. That's the magic of empathy. It brings more understanding. And understanding brings patience. And patience brings grace. And what marriage has an over-abundance of grace? None that we know of.

Grace primes the pump for the unnatural act of forgiveness.

Exercise 17: Walking in Your Partner's Shoes

When was the last time you consciously worked to see the world from your partner's perspective? If you are like most husbands and wives, it has been far too long. And your marriage is paying the price. This workbook exercise will help you hone your empathy skills and bring this valuable skill back into your relationship.

Forgiveness—Healing the Hurts You Don't Deserve

A husband and wife who have taken ownership for the good as well as the bad, who have planted a seed of hope by believing that good wins over bad, and who have dared to walk in each other's shoes in order to see that the bad is not as bad as they thought—this couple is light years ahead of the masses of married people. But they will not likely survive without a heavy dose of forgiveness.

The failure to give or receive forgiveness probably accounts for nearly every marriage that does not endure. How can two people who have so much opportunity to step on each other's toes survive without saying, "I'm sorry"? Yet in our counseling work, we have found that many husbands and wives have a hard time knowing when and how to say these words. They don't know when forgiveness is appropriate.

Most married people believe it's good to forgive and bad to hold on to grudges. But this can lead some people to forgive too easily. They become trigger-happy forgivers in order to one-up their spouse, as a way of making them feel guilty. Or they forgive quickly to avoid the pain. They think, *I'll put up with this horrible treatment because I don't know what I'll have without it*. Either way, rapid-fire forgiveness is unhealthy. And it is certainly not what forgiving is for.

Other people mistakenly take the opposite approach with forgiveness. They hold on to their forgiveness for fear they may run out. *After all*, they reason, *it doesn't make sense to give pardon to the person who has caused us deep pain*. What they don't know is that the main reason for forgiveness is what it does for the forgiver. Carrying rage against our partner does more harm to us than to them. That's why "the first and often

> Mutual empathy is the great unsung human gift.
> *Jean Baker Miller*

the only person to be healed by forgiveness, is the person who does the forgiving," says Lewis Smedes. "When we genuinely forgive, we set a prisoner free and then discover that the prisoner we set free was us."[6]

To forgive is to withhold judgment, forswear vengeance, renounce bitterness, break the silence of estrangement, and actually wish the best for the person who has hurt us. Forgiveness is not for the faint-hearted. Our sense of justice usually recoils at the thought of this unnatural act. Only the brave forgive.

In a good marriage, two people help one another become better at forgiving by asking for forgiveness when convicted, as well as by giving it when needed. *I'm sorry. Will you forgive me?* These simple words offer a possible way out of the inevitable blame game that traps so many couples.

"Where's my white shirt you said you'd pick up from the cleaners?" says the husband.

"I never said I'd get your shirt."

"I can't believe you."

"Don't pass the blame to me, it's your shirt."

"Yes, but I asked you last night to pick it up for me. Why didn't you?"

"You're crazy. We hardly even talked last night because you were at the game with Rick. Remember?"

"Oh, I get it. You didn't pick up my shirt because you're mad about me going to the game."

"Wait a second, who's the one who gets mad if I'm not home to make dinner every night?"

This inane dialogue bleats on and on until, at last, one partner says, "I'm sorry. Will you forgive me?" In the daily grind that is sometimes marriage, forgiveness keeps us moving forward.

> Love is an act of endless forgiveness, a tender look which becomes a habit.
>
> *Peter Ustinov*

But for some agonizing couples, a devastating hurt—one that was completely undeserved and goes against God's moral grain—calls on forgiveness to do much more than that. Sometimes in a good marriage, a pain of betrayal has cut so deep that forgiveness is the only thing between this couple and their demise. Forgiveness is their last hope for keeping them from their finale. Can it do so? Is it fair to ask so much of forgiveness? Yes, indeed. Forgiveness was designed to do this and only this: to heal the deepest wounds of a human heart.

> In the ideal marriage husband and wife are not loyal to each other because it is their duty, but because it is their joy.
>
> E. Merrill Root

Untold marriages have been saved by little more than forgiveness. Just ask Gordon Mc-Donald, pastor of Trinity Baptist Church in New York City. "I had horribly offended God and those whom I loved the most," he writes. "They had every right to turn their backs on me and hold me hostage to anger."[7] His betrayal of his wife brought their marriage to the ragged edge of its darkest abyss, and the only thing that kept them from tumbling in was his humble repentance and his wife's brave forgiveness.[8]

The most creative power in the soul of any marriage is the power to heal the hurts one didn't deserve. Forgiveness allows transformation in the guilty party and healing in the person who has been wronged.

In addition to breaking the cycle of blame and loosening the stranglehold of guilt, forgiveness does something else for a good marriage. It puts both partners on the same side of the fence, or perhaps it tears the fence down altogether. Through forgiveness, we realize we're not as different from the wrongdoer as we'd like to think. And that is what calls every couple to commitment.

Real-Life Problem Solvers

How We Found Forgiveness
after an Affair

Richard and Linda Simons
Married in 1970

We were on a fast track right from the beginning—so fast it eventually got reckless. Richard had started his own advertising agency; we were making lots of money, buying expensive cars, living large. It seemed there was nothing we couldn't do or have. And for me (Richard), that included women. Early in our marriage, I began a series of liaisons that eventually shattered the very core of our marriage. For more than five years, I betrayed Linda by seeing other women and deluded myself into thinking it didn't matter. That all changed on a Saturday in September when we sat down and talked honestly for the first time as husband and wife. I confessed my womanizing, and Linda, pregnant with our second child, demanded a divorce.

Richard's Experience

I was one of the most self-centered and irresponsible husbands you could find. As an entrepreneur, I approached everything in my life on my own terms, with no accountability to anyone. As I was growing my business and enjoying the accoutrements of success, I saw women as just another conquest, another trophy. I lied to Linda to be with other women. I sought them out, structuring my day and time around them. I wooed women for the fun of it. A night. A week. It didn't matter. It was all about me and my deceptive lifestyle. I was living a lie.

Linda's Experience

Richard was becoming more and more absorbed in his career, and I was becoming desperately lonely. The more success he had, the more left out I felt. Eventually I put the pieces together. He was spending inordinate amounts of time at the office on evenings and weekends, and it became apparent to me that something was going on other than meeting with clients. He came in at all hours of the night with very weak excuses to explain his absences. In my heart I knew he was being unfaithful. He had little interest in a sexual relationship with me, he criticized me constantly, and he was more or less pursuing his own life, not ours.

How We Solved the Problem

Our defining moment came when Richard confessed his womanizing and was repentant. That very day we called a minister, who counseled us on the phone at length. The next day we were in church—a place we hadn't been for quite some time. There we began to overhaul our lives. Eventually, I (Linda) decided our marriage was worth fighting for, and I dropped my threats of divorce. I had regretfully considered aborting our baby; I dropped that too.

We got out of the fast lane, made new friends, and began putting the pieces of our life back together. For me, that meant learning to forgive Richard. What he had done had hurt my heart to the very core. I didn't know if I could ever forgive him. We entered counseling and worked on new ways to communicate. We picked up new skills for getting along. But all the while, my heart was working at mending itself and letting go of the pain Richard had caused. I don't know the precise time or day I reached forgiveness, but somewhere in that year of recovery, my wounded heart, by God's grace, made room for Richard once again.

And I (Richard) began my own journey of reform. I brought accountability into my life. I surrounded myself and our marriage with positive people. I made our marriage my top priority. I learned how to honor Linda and how to prize our times of romance. We attended marriage seminars and more marriage counseling. We did everything we could think to do. But mostly, our marriage survived this hellish time because of forgiveness. It has become the lifeblood of our relationship.

A Word to Other Couples

You can survive almost anything with the forgiveness that comes when you open your heart to God's amazing grace.

Commitment—Living the Love You Promise

"For better or for worse, for richer or poorer, in sickness and in health, until death do us part." Just words. A mere phrase, really. You hear them at every wedding. Are you impressed? Probably not. It's one thing to say these words; it's another to keep them. Let's face it, this promise can only be proven over the course of a lifetime. And half of the time it is broken.

We had assembled a small panel of marriage experts to interview in front of an auditorium of nearly 200 college students studying marriage at our university. None of these experts had a Ph.D. They'd never published scholarly articles or anything else related to marriage. We don't even know if they'd ever read a single article on matrimony. All we knew is that these couples were experts by virtue of the longevity of their relationships. Elvin and Lois, married seventy-two years. Ken and Mable, sixty-eight years. Eldon and Dotty, seventy.

"Did you know marriages could last so long?" we asked our students in opening the floor for their questions. They sat in awe of these affectionate couples, like they were viewing a rare curiosity that belongs in a museum. One student raised his hand to break the ice: "If you combine the number of years each of these couples have been married, it comes to 210." Students chuckled, but they got deadly quiet when the next student asked, "What has kept you together all these years?"

> Marriage is three parts love and seven parts forgiveness of sins.
> Langdon Mitchell

Elvin was the first one to speak up. "An abiding determination to do so," he said. The rest of the panel nodded in agreement.

Bill Lake would have agreed as well, if he had been present. Bill is a 103-year-old married man in Yakima, Washington, who has proved his pledge of commitment like few others. He does so unfailingly every day, sitting next to his wife, Gladys, in her convalescent center and watching her body slowly shut down from the ravages of Parkinson's disease. Her hands once shook with the disease, but now they have gone still. Her speech in healthier times was fluid, but she is now mute. Her face, which used to light up at seeing her husband, now is frozen.

"It isn't very pleasant for me or her," Bill says. "But what can you do?" What Bill does is pure dedication. He sits in the chair next to Gladys's bed for four hours a day, a visit in the morning and another in the afternoon. He passes the time reading to her, talking about their life together, or simply sitting—making good on the promise he made seventy-two years ago.

When he arrives for each of his visits, Bill brushes back Gladys's silver hair and greets her with a kiss on the head and a soothing voice. "Hi, sweetie. Can you hear me?" Her eyes just roll.

For better or worse. You better believe it. Bill has been visiting his wife in the convalescent center for nearly ten years. In that time he's seen people drop off relatives and never return. He's seen people die lonely. But he promises that won't happen to his wife while he's alive. We have a strong feeling he's right.

The "till death do us part" aspect of marriage is not an untouchable ideal but a living reality that is insured by an unswerving commitment—a willful agreement to keep love alive. And, no matter how long a couple has been married, commitment may be the most effective tool good marriages use in battling bad things. Without commitment and the trust it engenders, marriages would have no hope of enduring.

Dr. Scott Stanley, at the Center for Marital and Family Studies at the University of Denver, has probably done more to help us understand what commitment is and how it works than anyone we know. After years of research, he has concluded that the term *commitment* is generally used in two ways.

The first involves *constraint* and engenders feelings of obligation. It keeps a couple married, not because their hearts are necessarily in it, but because they gave their word.

The second aspect to commitment involves *dedication* and engenders enthusiasm and involvement. It translates into active devotion to one another and to the marriage. It's no surprise that studies show dedicated couples battle bad things better than couples who are committed only out of constraint.[9]

> Marriage is a commitment— a decision to do, all through life, that which will express love for one's spouse.
>
> *Herman H. Kieval*

The movie *City Slickers* provides an example of dedication in the character played by Billy Crystal. He is presented with a scenario by his friend Ed, also a married man.

"Let's say a spaceship lands and the most beautiful woman you ever saw gets out," Ed says. "All she wants to do is have the greatest sex in the universe with you. And the second it's over, she flies away for eternity. No one will ever know. And you're telling me you wouldn't do it?"

"No. What you're describing actually happened to my cousin Ronald. And his wife *did* find out about it at the beauty parlor. They know everything there."

"Forget about it!"

"Look, Ed, what I'm saying is it wouldn't make it all right if Barbara didn't know. *I'd* know. And I wouldn't like myself. That's all."

Some people approach commitment like Ed, looking for loopholes or ways to get around it. They feel trapped by their restraining commitment, rather than empowered by their devotion. The question then is not whether you and your partner are committed, but do you have the right kind of commitment?

Every marriage is held together, to some degree, out of restraint: the moral compunctions against divorce, the welfare of children, financial considerations, and so on. Constraints are just a fact of marriage, and they aren't bad. Don't think in terms of abolishing constraints; rather, look at ways to increase your devotion. Dedication combined with constraint is what Scott Stanley calls the "epoxy glue" of marriage—a superstrong bond created from mixing two powerful compounds.

That, after all, is the point of our wedding vows. Too many good couples have misunderstood the nature of vows. They thought their vows were an expression of their feelings for one another, a prediction of what their feelings would be in the future. But the very opposite is true. Vows are promises made for the times when the ecstasy of feeling in love is *not* present. Vows are not dependent on feelings, but on a commitment to work on the relationship, to remain faithful, regardless of feelings.

Everybody knows marriage is no picnic. At least not always. And even when it is, it sometimes rains. "Ants will sting, mosquitoes will bite, and you will get indigestion from the potato

salad," as Ruth Senter puts it. "But you will say 'Forever,' because love is a choice you have made."

Real-Life Problem Solvers

How We've Stayed Committed

Jeff and Stacy Kemp
Married in 1983

We never expected marriage to be easy. But then again, we never expected it to be all that tough, either. But it was. Right off the bat we ran headfirst into a major personality clash, and it's now into its second decade. As a result, we've had more irritations and quarrels with each other than we care to admit. At times it feels like we are more divided than united. Suffice it to say that we've each had cause to wonder why we married someone so different. We've each had times when we could have questioned our commitment. But we didn't. We've hung in there, through thick and thin, not for the kids (although that's vital), but because we value lifelong love. We value marriage, its sanctity and its purpose. We value commitment. And because of that, our marriage is better than ever.

Jeff's Experience

Compared to Stacy, I'm very impulsive. I like to do most things spur of the moment. I'm not into details. I don't need a date book to tell me when and if I can do what I want. If my work didn't demand it, I could go weeks without a schedule. Not Stacy. Her life runs like a Swiss clock. We are night and day different in our personalities, and both of us are dominant in our styles. And that has been the source of most of our tension.

When our first of four boys was born, the level of tension in our home hit a new peak. As I look back on it, I realize now that I was insensitive. As one boy became two, three, then four, Stacy was working like mad to run our household the way she needed it to run while I, more or less, sat on the sidelines and watched. I didn't understand her approach, and she didn't understand mine. But that never caused me to question our commitment.

Stacy's Experience

Compared to Jeff, I'm very organized and even somewhat compulsive, but I rely on that to run a household of four boys—five, if you count Jeff! Do I get frustrated with Jeff for not being more understanding? You bet. And I get frustrated about him not being more like me. We have such differing styles. We approach almost everything from a different perspective. He likes to socialize on a big scale; I enjoy a more intimate evening with friends. I'm objective; he's subjective. I like to live by a schedule, and he likes to fly by the seat of his pants. Sure, Jeff and I have both been changing for the better over the years, but we are still a long way from seeing everything eye-to-eye. But that has never brought into question whether we would work on this relationship and stay committed to one another.

How We've Stayed Committed

Let's make this point clear: Divorce has never entered our vocabulary. Neither of us consider it an option to our troubles. We've seen plenty of couples who trade in one set of marriage problems for a new set of problems after divorce. That's not for us. Our picture of marriage has never included a hint of throwing in the towel. We are here for the long run to make this relationship work. Of

course, this takes faith—in each other, and in God. We are only together today as husband and wife because we both rely on God to see us through.

I (Jeff) have worked hard to understand the differences between men and women. I've worked hard to understand Stacy and our differing styles. And I (Stacy) have worked hard to appreciate and affirm Jeff. But in spite of our best efforts, we fail continually to love each other the way we want. That's why the strength of our commitment rests on God, not ourselves. And that's why joy far outweighs the frustrations in our marriage.

A Word to Other Couples

Erase divorce from your vocabulary and allow a bright picture of your future together to shape your attitudes, your choices, and your actions today.

As we said at the start, if your marriage has ran into some problems, your journey toward regaining the good you fear losing may not be speedy or smooth. But, in time, you are sure to reach your destination if you . . .

take responsibility for the good as well as the bad,

believe that good wins over bad,

walk in your partner's shoes,

work to heal the hurts you don't deserve, and

live the love you promise.

So don't be discouraged. You're probably closer than you think. "Many of life's failures," said Thomas Edison, "are people who did not realize how close they were to success when they gave up."

For Reflection

1. Do you agree that problems can only be overcome by a couple when they each take responsibility for their own attitudes and actions? Can you recall a specific time when you did this in your marriage? What was the result?
2. Some experts have said that hope is not an ethereal thing some people have made it out to be. It is about having concrete goals. What do you think? Have you found it productive to formalize your hopes for your marriage into goals?
3. How often would you say you consciously put yourself in your partner's shoes? Can you think of a time when empathy changed your perspective on something in your marriage?
4. Forgiveness is truly a radical method of restoration. Looking back over your married life, can you identify times when forgiveness that you either gave or received changed the course of your relationship? How so?

———

Marriage is our last, best chance to grow up.
Joseph Barth

———

joining your spirits like never before

Deep down in the soul of your marriage
is a thirst for connection that can only be quenched
when you drink from the ultimate source of love.

Marriage calls for faith of the most radical sort.
Elizabeth Cody Newenhuyse

We moved from Seattle to Oklahoma City last week. It's not a permanent move. But for the next twelve months we will live in this city and work with the governor's office on one of the nation's most innovative and surprising social programs.

After Nevada, you see, Oklahoma has the highest divorce rate in the nation. Right here in what some describe as the buckle of the Bible belt, marriages are crumbling at alarming rates. Surprised? You're not the only one. In fact, you are in the same company as the state's governor.

Speculations on why Oklahoma would have such a disturbing divorce rate are many. But Governor Frank Keating is not waiting passively for social scientists to pinpoint answers. He and the First Lady are doing something radical. In an all-out, unprecedented move, the Keatings formed the first ever statewide marriage initiative with a bold goal: to reduce the divorce rate in Oklahoma by a third in the next ten years. What's more, the governor has devoted ten million dollars to make it happen. No governor in U.S. history has ever focused more energy—or money—on marriage.

So when we received a call inviting us to be part of such an unprecedented undertaking to build better marriages throughout an entire state, we didn't have to think twice. As the governor's "marriage ambassadors" for the next year, it is our job to raise the public level of awareness about marriage and to equip as many couples as possible for lifelong love. This assignment, of course, is not without its challenges. Already, in the short time we have been here, we have discovered many sincere couples with no more preparation for marriage than a wing and a prayer. Literally. Many couples we encounter are relying almost entirely on God to keep them happily married. "God brought us together and he's going to keep us together," a cheerful bride told us just yesterday.

In a state that has a church on nearly every corner, couples cling to their faith as the bedrock of their relationship. And yet with such a good religious foundation, their relationships are turning bad—so bad that there are more divorces than marriages in most counties.

The question on every conscientious mind is *why?* Why would couples who believe in and depend on God for strength in their marriage have seemingly no advantage over those who enter marriage without a Christian conviction?

> Life's setbacks are temporary, but God's love is permanent. He's always there to take us over the rough spots, to lead us out of our slumps and into our grooves.
>
> *Terry Pendleton*

We're convinced the answer lies deep in the soul of every aching marriage. At the center of our shared lives, underneath the layers of everydayness, a tension mounts for even the most committed couples whose restless spirits have not been nourished by God *together*. It is a slow-growing tension, for most, not easily described. It spawns a rest-lessness that only exacerbates the ache we feel in our marriage. But it is there, in that yearning ache to walk with God, and in our confession that we've never felt so out of step with our Creator together, that we begin to find healing. In other words, the ease for the ache in the soul of our marriage is found in a soul-to-soul connection with each other as we relate to God.

A Quick Tale of Two Marriages

A good marriage cannot survive on love alone, as we pointed out in an earlier chapter. And at the risk of sounding almost heretical, believing in God is not enough to make a marriage good. Consider two similar but distinct marriages: One is the marriage of two sincere believers whose individual faiths have never really commingled. They have never gone beneath the sur-face of the perfunctory behaviors that religion requires, and as a result their spiritual connection is nothing more than window dressing on a relationship that is aching for more. While they both believe in God individually, they have never related to God as a couple—not in any meaningful fashion. That's why they feel more like roommates than soul mates.

The other is a marriage of two people whose faith is fresh. They may struggle with doubts and spiritual dry spells, but on the whole, they are on a positive spiritual path. Individually, they seek to know God and follow Jesus. But unlike so many church-going couples, these two have found ways to interact with each other on the spiritual plane, even in the midst of their fast-paced lives. Their individual spirituality is inspired by the sacred moments, be they ever so fleeting, that they share as a couple. Their religious behaviors are not mere rituals or duties; they are meaningful activities that bring them deep below the surface of the daily grind and then enable them to soar on the wings of shared spiritual experiences.

Because you are still reading this chapter, we believe you share the longing of countless couples to find the serenity for your soul and the joy for your spirit that this couple enjoys.

So we devote this chapter to every couple who is longing for a deeper connection. It is for those of us who aren't willing to settle for a superficial shared faith. This chapter is for all of us who dare to share life's ultimate meaning with our soul mate and discover the oneness that only a shared commitment to spiritual discovery can bring.

Who's More Interested?

There are two major reasons couples get out of sync spiritually. The first is due to an uneven level of interest in spirituality itself. Let's be honest: As two unique human beings with differing needs, differing backgrounds, differing dispositions, and differing interests, it is only natural that we will have differing desires to discuss spiritual issues. In nearly every marriage, one partner leans more heavily on spiritual conversations than the other. Even in marriages between two sincere, churchgoing people, one partner will want to get lost in deep conversations about God, while the other is content simply to share activities like going to church. One partner wants to pray lengthy, intimate prayers with his or her spouse, while the other is content to simply say grace at the dinner table.

Why the difference? A multitude of reasons. Perhaps the more-interested spouse is experiencing a spiritual "growth spurt" while the less-interested partner is on a plateau. Maybe the more-interested spouse grew up in a home where spiritual issues were discussed more often. Or maybe the less-interested spouse is more introverted in general than the partner who is more expressive and vulnerable about *all* areas of his or her life. Or maybe the less-interested partner feels manipulated into a spiritual role that does not feel natural or genuine. There are many reasons for an uneven level of spiritual interests between partners. But whatever the reason, over time, as the dichotomy of differences seems more and more pronounced for some couples, a deadly potion of two major ingredients is brewing. Disappointment on one side and guilt on the other mix to create a powerful saboteur of spiritual intimacy. It is a bitter drink that too many couples swig as their spirits collide. Eventually, these couples give up on spiritual intimacy and give in to the chronic ache of their marital soul.

If you find yourself identifying with the unequal interest quotient, allow us to speak to you individually.

First, to the more-interested spouse: Ease up. Whether you are doing it intentionally or not, your partner probably feels judged by your eagerness to make a deep, spiritual connection. And the more guilt he or she feels, the tougher it is for a genuine change to take place. Instead of focusing on how you can have a spiritual conversation or a time of prayer together, take a different tack. Gently end conversations about spiritual matters when you notice your mate is withdrawing or becoming uncomfortable. It's better to try again later than to cause frustration by pressing to keep alive a conversation that's going nowhere. And when your partner does add spiritual input to your marriage, express your appreciation. Let him or her know how much it means to you. This affirmation goes a long way toward easing your spouse's discomfort and increasing his or her spiritual expressiveness.

> The story of a love is not important. What is important is that one is capable of love. It is perhaps the only glimpse we are permitted of eternity.
>
> *Helen Hayes*

To the less-interested spouse: Be real. Examine what your heart is telling you. If you are feeling pressured, guilty, or angry, say so. If you try to bury these negative emotions, they will resurface later when you are merely going through the motions. This does not mean, of course, that you put any and all of your negative feelings about these issues on your spouse, but it does mean that you confess them to God—in private. Once you cleanse your heart of these spiritual toxins, share your fears and uneasiness with your spouse as best you can. This is easier than you might think. Write a letter if it helps. Include the reasons you find it difficult to discuss your spiritual life (maybe your upbringing has shaped this, for example). Don't assume your mate knows these things. And finally, recognize your important role. When it comes to spiritual intimacy, there is something your spouse values deeply that only you can give. Though talking about spiritual matters may not come easily to you, this is a gift you can give when you are ready.

Admitting, as a couple, the unequal spiritual interest you have in your marriage is the first step toward finding improvement. The next step comes in learning a new spiritual language—your partner's.

Speaking Your Spouse's Spiritual Language

One of the single biggest stumbling blocks to spiritual intimacy in a marriage is a failure to understand and appreciate the other's spiritual language. In other words, if we don't recognize that our partner's means of communion with God is valid, we discount it. Intentionally or not, we send a message to our partner that says *you don't know God like I do.*

A kindergarten teacher was observing her classroom of children while they drew. She would occasionally walk around to see each child's artwork. As she got to one little girl who was working diligently, she asked what the drawing was. The girl replied, "I'm drawing God." The teacher paused and said, "But no one knows what God looks like." Without missing a beat or looking up from her drawing, the girl replied, "They will in a minute."

We sometimes come to our view of God and how to relate to him in a similar fashion. We focus so much on how *we* see God that we expect everyone else—especially our spouse—to see him the very same way. And that's a terrible mistake for most married couples since there are a number of equally valid pathways for expressing our love of God.

Some time ago, we were speaking at Willow Creek Community Church in Barrington, Illinois. Bill Hybels, the pastor of this great church, told us about a book that has since helped us greatly in our desire to deepen our own level of spiritual intimacy as a couple. So much so, that we feel compelled to share the gist of its message with you. The book is *Sacred Pathways* by Gary Thomas. Though the book was not written with couples in mind, we immediately saw the application of Thomas's message to easing the soul-searching ache so many couples experience. In fact, we recently talked with Gary Thomas about this, and he was quick to confess that his own marriage was the catalyst for his thinking. "I knew my wife loved God," he said, "but I didn't understand why she didn't relate to him the way I did."

The message of Thomas's book is quite simple: Spirituality is not "one-size-fits-all."[1] There is a wonderful variety of ways to relate to God that are equally compelling. Gary unfolds several distinct spiritual temperaments that we have adapted and adjusted to be of particular relevance to couples. As you read about each one, consider where you see yourself and the ways you most naturally move toward God. Then think about how

> May we two live our lives so happily together that God may enjoy our union of heart and spirit with each other.
>
> *Ancient marriage prayer*

your partner might use one or more of these pathways more naturally than you.

The Pathway of Tradition

These people love God through rituals, sacraments, and symbols. Their life of faith is marked by disciplines and structure. They may read daily from a devotional text or have a routine time of kneeling in prayer. Others may view their pathway to God as legalistic, but traditionalists define their faith largely by their conduct. They enjoy regular church attendance, keeping the Sabbath, and observing rituals that have been passed down through the generations. Experiencing the same ritual week after week deepens their understanding and their commitment to God.

The Pathway of Vision

These people love God by dreaming a great dream. They have their mind set on the future and are focused on what can be. They are energized by a mission that allows them to be part of something big, something that will result in bringing others to a deeper relationship with God. Visionaries are not content to sit still when they could be gathering the troops and pointing them in a better direction. They feel closest to God when they are a part of something big on his behalf.

The Pathway of Relationships

These people love God best by being around other people. They may struggle to pray on their own in private, but when they get with their prayer group they can't be stopped. They are energized by the socializing that happens in a church foyer and are often the last to leave after a service. They reach out to others by planning gatherings that include them. They feel closest to God when they are with people who love God too.

The Pathway of Intellectual Thought

These people seek God with their minds. They study to better know and understand ideas and models that bring them—and perhaps the people they teach—closer to God. They love the world of ideas and concepts. Faith, for them, is something to be analyzed and understood as much as experienced. They feel closest to God when they are reading a stimulating book that brings them fresh understanding of something related to God or the spiritual life.

The Pathway of Service

These people love God by loving others. They are drawn to people in need, and the more needs they meet, the more energized they feel. Quiet contemplation or energetic causes do little for their generous spirit. They are too busy interacting with the hungry, the ill, and the forgotten to focus much of their time on religious traditions and liturgical experiences. Caregivers feel closest to God when they are helping those who are in desperate need of help, whether they be right next door or halfway around the world.

The Pathway of Contemplation

These people seek to love God in a quiet pursuit. They are not wanting to explain God with intellectual concepts as much as they are simply seeking to be near him. They listen to God through private times of meditation and prayer. The contemplative rests in God's presence. As Gary Thomas puts it, "Time is one of the best gifts we can give God, and contemplatives want to give God plenty."

The Pathway of Activism

These people are at war with injustice. Typically, they adopt either social or evangelistic causes and feel quite comfortable with confrontation. They are even energized by tough situations as they take their stand against evil in this world. They resonate with Jesus when he cleansed the temple, and they aspire to change the world with their heartfelt convictions. Activists feel closest to God when they are fighting for a cause.

The Pathway of Nature

These people feel closest to God in the outdoors. Whether they are walking through the woods, enjoying an open meadow, or hiking up a mountain, these believers are moved by creation. "They learn more from looking at a peaceful lake than from reading a book or listening to a sermon," says Thomas. Naturalists see God best by surrounding themselves with his beautiful creation.

The Pathway of Worship

These people are inspired by joyful celebration. Thomas calls them "cheerleaders for God." They enter worship by clapping their hands, shouting "Amen!" and dancing in their excitement. They don't need the rituals of the traditionalist or the solitude of the contemplative as much as they need to celebrate the glory of God. Their playful and childlike spirit shines as they delight in celebrative songs of enthusiastic worship.

Exercise 18: Assessing Your Spiritual Language

After reading through these several spiritual pathways to God, you are probably wondering which one not only best fits your temperament, but also that of your spouse. If so, this workbook exercise will help you shed some light on your two styles. Whether you think you already have your spouse "diagnosed" or not, this exercise will help the two of you constructively discuss your potentially divergent styles.

Real-Life Problem Solvers

How We Learned to Speak the Same Spiritual Language

Chuck and Barb Snyder
Married in 1955

Barb and I are the "World's Most Opposite Couple." As we often say, we have only two things in common: We were married on the same day, and we have the same kids. We are especially opposite when it comes to spirituality. When we first married, I always felt Barb was more "spiritual" than me. She enjoyed studying her Bible, while I didn't see how the Bible was very relevant to my life. I was more eager to roll up my sleeves and put the Bible into practice. I felt closer to God, in fact, when I was helping other people.

It's true, I (Barb) had a consuming desire to know what the Bible had to say. I would put the children to bed early and pore over the Scriptures until bedtime. Chuck was working swing shift at a television station, so he wasn't around in the evening and didn't have a clue what I was doing. Whenever I shared something that I learned, Chuck almost always argued with me. You have to know Chuck to know that he always has a different opinion anyway. I used to dream of having a meaningful and pleasant discussion about God with him. But this always seemed elusive.

Chuck's Experience

Early in our marriage I thought I was a spiritual misfit. And I was plagued by guilt. Looking back, I had been mistaught

about what it meant to be the "spiritual leader" of a home.
I thought I had to be in charge of all the "spiritual stuff" in
the family. Then someone showed me Matthew 20, where
Jesus pointed out that being the head of a family, a business, or a ministry, was to be a servant. God used his Son
as a supreme example. He came to earth and washed
people's feet. This had never been my idea of a leader.
Ephesians 5 then comes along and says, "Husbands, love
your wives, just as Christ loved the church and gave himself up for her." That's when I realized something spiritual
had been amiss in our marriage.

Barb's Experience

In the early 1970s Kay Arthur showed me how to study
inductively, starting with the Bible first before reading
commentaries or other outside sources. One day I had my
Greek study helps and a precept workbook spread out on
the kitchen table when Chuck walked by. He tapped the
books and said, "This really intimidates me." *Great,* I
thought to myself, *he not only doesn't appreciate me talking about Scripture; he doesn't want to see me study it.* I
knew Chuck was trying to be a spiritual leader in our
home, but he wasn't leading the way I wanted. All I
wanted was to study God's Word together. He didn't see
it that way.

How We Solved the Problem

We took our first steps toward solving our spiritual
dilemma when somehow, somewhere, we came to realize
that we had different spiritual gifts. Chuck's is exhorta-
tion. He loves coming alongside people and giving them
encouragement and counsel. My spiritual gift is teaching.
I love to reveal new truths and help another person gain
fresh insight. This simple revelation in our marriage began

a revolution in our hearts. For the first time, I realized Chuck didn't have to study like *I* did. And he realized that I didn't have to enjoy counseling others like *he* did. Chuck could be who he is, and I could be who I am. Knowing this put a virtual end to our arguing about spiritual matters. We started to value each other's gifts and speak each other's language. This was refreshing for both of us. Chuck could now relax in our relationship and didn't have to be intimidated by me as a teacher. To this very day, he tells me that I provide the biblical foundation upon which he stands as he helps hurting people.

A Word to Other Couples

Let your partner be who God designed them to be and then learn from each other.

Building Your Spiritual House

There you have it. Nine spiritual pathways to God. If you have taken the time to do the self-assessment in the workbook, you have identified which styles fit you and your partner best. So now what? Well, now comes the daring part. This is where the two of you explore and understand each other's differing pathways. This is where the two of you begin to work together to appreciate each other's spiritual language. And as you do, you will build a new "spiritual house"—one where the ache in the soul of your marriage begins to dissipate.

Be forewarned, however, the house you build will probably not be the one you have envisioned. As you explore and learn one another's spiritual language, as you appreciate and incorporate your spouse's pathway into yours, you will build a spiritual house that combines—sometimes oddly—your potentially divergent styles.

About thirty miles from Belfast, Northern Ireland, close to the shore of Strangford, Lough, is a stately home that tourists can visit called Castleward. It is a good physical representation of what we are talking about. The house was built in the 1760s, and its original owners were Bernard Ward, the first viscount of Bangor, and his wife, Lady Anne.

The most striking feature of the house is its display of two different styles of architecture. The rear of the house is Gothic, while the front is neoclassical. Bernard enjoyed one style while Lady Anne another. Today, the house still stands—as a monument to stubbornness, some would say, but to others, it is a celebration of diversity.

Like we said, the combination of your spiritual styles may make for an interesting design. It has for us.

A Work in Progress

For most of our marriage, we have been out of sync with each other in how we relate to God. We started out with good intentions to make a meaningful spiritual connection between us, but somewhere in our first year we ended up on relatively divergent paths. Not that we didn't share the same values. Not that we didn't maintain our individual walks with God. And not that we didn't both want a deep spiritual connection with each other. It was more that we didn't understand each other's attempts to relate to God individually, and that made it seemingly impossible to relate to God together as a couple. But as we are learning, it all comes down to knowing, and then affirming, each other's spiritual style.

Leslie's Spiritual Style: I am a contemplative, through and through. I like nothing more than to spend a couple hours each day alone with God. Having a toddler at my feet has put a crimp in my style, but this still remains my primary pathway to God. I have had the same prayer book for years and the same well-worn Bible too. They keep me company as I seek to love God with the purest and deepest love I can. I've been doing this since college. Even as a freshman, I awoke early, before my roommate, to enjoy the quiet morning hours as I spent time with God. This wasn't out of duty. It wasn't a discipline I worked at. It came quite naturally.

Nothing about this style seemed natural to Les, however. He saw it as too time-consuming and unproductive.

Les's Spiritual Style: I am an intellectual. I don't know if it's in my blood—I share this style with some family members—or if my years of academic training (including seminary) set me on this path. Whatever the reason, I feel closest to God when I am learning a new truth. If I can conceptualize some aspect of the Christian life in a new or fresh way, if I can wrap my mind around a truth, I come alive in my relationship with God. The time I most often spend with God is while I'm reading a new book or working in my study, lined with reference tools that help me in my spiritual pursuit. Not so for Leslie. She viewed my approach as too academic and emotionally removed.

> Sometimes—as in peeling onions— we cry so hard we can't see what we're doing. But I don't give up onions for that reason. Nor will I give up you.
>
> *Jana Carman*

So where are we now? Both of us are still walking the paths that bring us, as individuals, closer to God. But both of us are also placing value on each other's style. This is new. We used to each expect the other to conform more to our individual leanings. After all, we each felt this was the best way to relate to God. And it is—for us individually. But not as a couple. This simple truth has been a breakthrough for our marriage. It is allowing us to meld our methods and try on some new approaches that neither of us is naturally drawn to. Lately, for example, we have been learning from some fellow worshipers. We are joining in worship with praise music like never before. It has been a wonderful point of connection for us as we relate to God together.

I (Leslie) am not expecting Les to wake early so he can enjoy a quiet time with me; in fact, I'm learning how invigorating it can be to study a topic with Les in one of his commentaries. And I (Les) am learning the profound stirring in my heart that comes from a contemplative moment of doing nothing more than being with God. We are not converting each other to fit into a style that is not natural, but we are encouraging each other's means to God like we have never done in the past.

Expecting your spouse to relate to God with a certain style can wreak havoc in your marriage. God does not want us to become chameleons. He wants us to be real. He wants us to come to him in the most natural of ways. And so we must value and affirm the way our spouse relates to God, whether it be as a naturalist, a traditionalist, an activist, or something else.

People experience God by walking in the woods, singing songs of praise, shutting out the noise of the world, studying theology. And each practice awakens us to a new sense of spiritual vitality. As you embrace your partner's pathway, you will discover a part of your spirit that has never been touched before. You will discover something within you that draws you, your partner, and God closer than ever. And that's the turning point. That is when the ache in the soul of your marriage begins to ease.

Going Deeper: The God-Centered Marriage

We know a couple who celebrated their first anniversary with a romantic candlelit dinner at home. Near the end of the main course, the wife slipped away only to emerge from the kitchen with the perfect dessert for the finishing touch: the top of their wedding cake. With the first cut into the cake, however, both of them knew something was wrong. The cake squeaked. With a little more cutting, they discovered the problem. For an entire year, they had saved a round chunk of frosting-covered Styrofoam in their freezer.

Looks can be deceiving. As this silly but true story illustrates, we can focus so much on the

Patience in marriage works a lot like faith. It demonstrates the certainty that what we hope for — physical, emotional, spiritual oneness — is waiting for us, even though we cannot see it in the here and now.

Harold B. Smith

externals of a relationship that we neglect to see what we are actually preserving in our marriage. Which brings up a serious subject: Deep down, what do you believe is the core purpose of your marriage? To be happy? We trust you've learned by now that marriage was never designed to act as insurance against sadness. Good marriages, and even great ones, are by no means protected from bad things. So, we ask again. What is the central purpose of your marriage?

We have thought long and hard about this question, and here is our answer: The purpose of our marriage is to draw us closer to God. We used to think that God would help us draw closer to each other, that he would help us build a better marriage. And he does. But our emphasis in recent years has focused more on how our marriage helps us build a better relationship with God. This turnabout in thinking has revolutionized our relationship. Instead of asking God to help our marriage, we are more apt to ask each other how we can help the other walk closer to God. Marriage, in other words, is becoming an important means to our Creator. The challenges we face, the joys we celebrate — more than most anything — are bringing us into an intimate relationship with God.

Real-Life Problem Solvers

HOW WE FIND GOD'S WILL TOGETHER

Norm and Bobbe Evans
Married in 1961

The husband calls the shots. And the wife follows orders. Those beliefs sound incredibly old-fashioned and politically incorrect now, but that's what we believed when we got married. Both of us grew up in homes where Dad's decisions were final. His word was the law, and we hadn't seen our mothers try to amend it. So as a bride and groom of only seventeen and eighteen years of age, we fell into these strict roles without a second thought. Norm was the leader, and I (Bobbe) would go along with Norm's plans. Besides, he said he wanted to make me happy, and I thought that meant we'd always work things out equitably.

The honeymoon lasted pretty much through our college years. And when I (Norm) entered the pros, our roles were pretty well defined. I played football and Bobbe managed most everything at home. I can't even think of a time Bobbe questioned my wisdom or decisions—not until we had been married for nearly twenty years. I decided to start my own company and publish sports literature. A short time later, the venture failed, costing us everything we had been saving in all my fourteen years as a professional football player. This terrible time marked a turning point in our style of making decisions.

Norm's Experience

To say that football was my life when we got married would be an understatement. For six months out of the year, everything I did revolved around the game. From my eating to my sleeping, football was my focus. I literally had to force myself to pay attention to Bobbe and the kids. My macho image was a prerequisite to my job. I showed no fear. I was decisive. To succeed at my game, that's the way it had to be. So I carried the same bull-headed leadership style into my marriage. And it worked, for a time. But when our financial security fell out from under us, I had no one to blame but myself. I had never asked Bobbe for her advice. I didn't feel I needed it. But as my independent decision making got us into more and more trouble, I realized that there must be a better way.

Bobbe's Experience

I had a picture of what a good Christian wife should look like, and that picture did not include questioning my husband. I thought my role was to submit to his leadership . . . the old "chain-of-command." Norm and I became Christians as adults, and I was taught the husband was the head of the home and the wife was to be his helper. The ultimate decision was to be up to my husband. To continue to disagree with Norm, I thought, was not my place. It wasn't godly and it demeaned his leadership. Still, whenever I had expressed doubts or reservations about an issue and he went ahead anyway, I wanted to say, "I told you so." But I didn't. I bit my tongue when it came to reminding him of my advice while I swallowed my anger and resentment. But through the years, I came to see that this kind of stifling was not what God intended for my spirit or for our marriage. He had designed me with a brain, a voice, and a set of emotions, and he intended for me to use them.

How We Solved the Problem

Once we came to a place of knowing that our decision-making style had to change, we started a process that turned us around—a process that brought us closer to each other and closer to God. It began by realizing that some of the things we'd been taught were not right. We learned from writers and speakers with a new message about seeking God's will together as a couple (Ephesians 5:21). Out of that came a realization that guides our decisions to this day: God would not put us at odds with each other on any important decision. In other words, God would not touch Norm's heart to do something that would impact our marriage if he did not also touch my heart in a similar way.

Next, I (Norm) began to ask Bobbe for input on decisions I was considering. I looked back on some of the mistakes and remembered that she had given me good advice, which I had ignored. And I (Bobbe) had to learn a new style of giving my input. Our parents never modeled this, so we decided both of us could benefit from counseling. This was a huge step, especially for a macho football player. But in counseling we learned new ways to communicate. Our counselor gave us practice exercises to hone our listening skills. He taught us to speak "I" messages. We learned to ask for clarification of each other's intentions. This was hard work for both of us, and we had to practice, practice, practice. (Which an old football player knows how to do!)

Finally, we began to approach important decisions in a new way. We recognized and saw the value of how different we are. God has designed each of us uniquely and individually. We don't have to be exactly alike. In fact, if we don't agree on something, like an important decision in our work, we don't proceed with it until we do. This has raised our level of respect for each other tremendously. On important decisions, we also now ask other experts for input. God has a way of speaking through other people, and we listen with both ears. Most of all, we seek God's will as a couple as much as we do as individuals. And we trust God to direct our path—together.

A Word to Other Couples

Learning to make decisions together as a couple takes time and practice. Don't give up. God will reveal his desires to both of you as you learn to walk in step with him.

It may seem strange, but it is as though we have added to the list of historical spiritual disciplines, such as prayer, meditation, the study of Scripture, fasting, and so on, a new discipline: marriage. Yes, marriage. Once we realized that the core purpose of our marriage is to draw us closer to God, we began to view our relationship not as an end, but a means. We began to see that everything about our marriage, if we were willing to open our eyes, provides potential for discovering and revealing more of God. The times we forgive and seek grace from each other, the ecstasy of lovemaking, the laughter and fun we experience, our commitment and the shared history we create together—these and other facets of our marriage release God's nature in our lives. And married life has never been sweeter. A stronger marriage is a side effect of learning to love God—together.

Of course, we are not the first to discover this "new" view of marriage. In fact, it is an idea that's as old as Scripture. The Bible, remember, is filled with images of the bridegroom and the bride and of a husband with his wife. But for some reason, it has taken us years to figure this out for our own relationship. Maybe it's "new" to you too. Either way, we want to devote the remainder of this chapter to something special that will help you deepen your connection with God and each other. It is not so much a tool as it is an experience that will nurture the soul of your marriage.

Joining Your Spirits Like Never Before

"I can see your car right now," Les said. He was talking into his cell phone while standing in our driveway. "You just turned the corner and you'll be here any minute." We both began waving our arms to show Neil and Marylyn where we were. Baby John, our two-year-old, began jumping up and down beside us with excitement.

Neil and Marylyn Warren are two of our very favorite people. They were on a cross-country trek, just a few days ago, when they decided to go out of their way to stop by our house for a meal together. And they didn't come empty-handed. "Hey, John," Neil said to our baby, "we've got something for you." From the backseat of their car, Neil revealed a huge box containing a tricycle. John squealed with delight. "Nice," was the word this two-year-old selected from his limited vocabulary. "Nice." He said the word at least a dozen times. "Nice." John sat on his haunches as he watched Neil and Les use makeshift tools to assemble this toy on the floor of our living room. Once it was put together, John climbed aboard. "Nice."

And it was. So nice, in fact, we didn't want our time to end. We ate a leisurely lunch together (while John slept in my arms) at an Italian restaurant. The conversation, as always, was fun, meaningful, crazy, deep, vulnerable, and exciting, all mixed in together. They asked us questions about our future and helped us shape our vision through the conversation. As we heard them talk about their dreams, we found fuel for our own. Our marriage, right then and there, was infused with new energy. We must have sat around that table for at least three hours. Then, reluctantly, Neil and Marylyn had to get back on the road.

"What a great lunch," Les said as we walked out of the restaurant. We all agreed, and everyone knew we weren't talking about the food. Even now, we can't quite explain it, can't put our finger on it. But every time we're around these two and their time-tested marriage of several decades, we feel better. More enlightened, more in tune with each other. Maybe it's their contagious optimism. Maybe it's their sharp thinking. Maybe it's their light-hearted spirits. We don't know for sure. All we know is that they are an inspiration. Neil and Marylyn do something for us that few others can do so consistently. They inspire our marriage. We always feel like we have sprouted new wings as a couple when we are with them. And they have taught us an invaluable lesson in spiritual intimacy: Inspiration is what bonds two souls together and enables them to soar.[2]

So powerful is the gift of inspiration to the soul of your marriage that we felt we could not close this chapter without it. Whenever a husband and wife have an inspirational experience together, their spirits are joined at an indescribable depth. They come together on a level that normal existence never even considers. Inspiration peels away the mundane layers of our lives and causes us to look beyond our silly squabbles, self-seeking desires, and uncaring comments, and appreciate what matters most.

Exercise 19: Finding the Inspiration around You

You may not always know how to explain it, but you certainly know when it happens. Inspiration. It is invaluable to every couple wanting to find the fulfillment and contentment that comes from joining your spirits together. This exercise in the husband's and wife's workbooks will help you recall inspirational moments that have infused your marriage, and it will help you cultivate this quality more and more into your daily walk with each other and with God.

The Invigoration of Inspiration

Think about a movie that moved you. Have you ever sat in a theater or rented a movie that brought you both to tears? Have you ever read a novel or a biography that caused you both to reevaluate your lives? Perhaps you heard a song that was sung so exquisitely, so tenderly, or so boldly, that you never forgot it. Maybe you listened to a message that was so poignant that it pierced your collective hearts.

One of our most inspirational moments came when we least expected it. We were driving on the Trans-Canada Highway through Banff National Park in the world-famous Rocky Mountains when we thought we'd stay the night at a hotel near Lake Louise. Turns out we were not the only ones with this idea. At 10:00 P.M. when we checked at the registration desk of the beautiful Chateau Lake Louise, the man behind the desk told us that people typically scheduled their stays here at least a year in advance. There was not a single room available in the entire town, let alone his prestigious hotel. "Guess we'll sleep in the back of our Jeep," Les said.

"That's not a good idea. It gets extremely cold up here after dark," the bell captain chimed in.

The clerk apologized for our situation and suggested that we keep heading east on the highway. We were about to take his advice when we decided to enjoy a nice meal in the hotel's alpine dining room. After our dinner, Les decided to check with the clerk one last time.

"I can't believe this," the clerk exclaimed. "We have an opening. It is nearly midnight, and our guests have not arrived for the presidential suite; I can give it to you for the price of a normal room."

We were giddy with excitement as the bellman showed us to the expansive suite that included a grand veranda on the top two floors of the hotel. "Hope you enjoy the show," he said.

"What show?" I asked.

"Out your window," he replied. "It's the night of one hundred shooting stars."

He was right. We could not believe our eyes. Time stood still as we watched star after star fly across the black velvet night. We'd never heard of and certainly not seen such a sight before. No words can do it justice. "Amazing," was all we could say.

I'm not sure what time we fell asleep that night, but I know when we awoke. It was to the sound of a classic Swiss horn being played near the edge of the lake the next morning. And the song that was reverberating off the walls of ice and sheets of rock that circled the lake was "Amazing Grace." It was too much to behold. As we stood on the veranda looking out at the scene of a pristine lake we didn't know existed the night before, we stood silent. By the time the song was over, we each had tears brimming in our eyes. And that said it all. The inspiration of that moment will always be with us, permanently bonding us.

Inspiration does that. And allow us to quickly add that you

> Whenever inspiration graces your life together, recognize this as one of God's powerful ways of bonding you together so strongly that you can survive every twist of fate for as long as you live.
> *Neil Clark Warren*

do not have to be in an idyllic mountain setting to find it. We've shared inspirational moments watching a news report. We'll never forget the tragic scene of mistreated orphans in Romania and the story of one couple's quest to rescue and adopt a deformed little boy.

We've shared inspirational moments in worship. We'll never forget standing in a church and listening to Wayne Watson sing "For Such a Time as This." Our hearts have rarely been more full. Or the time we heard Lloyd John Ogilvie, now chaplain of the U.S. Senate, preach at Hollywood Presbyterian Church on "Finishing the Race." We felt our spirits soaring together.

And we've shared inspirational moments reading books together. Not long ago we read the memoirs of Christopher Reeve, the late *Superman* actor, who fell from a horse in a riding accident that severed his spinal cord and paralyzed him from the shoulders down. In the days which followed, both he and his mother considered pulling the plug on his life-support system. We got to the point in his book, *Still Me*, where he mouthed his first lucid words to Dana, his wife: "Maybe we should let me go." But his wife, through tears, persuaded him to fight back, saying, "I want you to know that I will be with you for the long haul, no matter what. You're still you, and I love you." Inspiration struck our marriage again.

What about you? When was the last time the two of you were inspired together? In case you don't know, there are countless inspirational moments waiting to be discovered by soul mates who are willing to find them. And when we do, our lives become richer, our connections deeper, and our spirits lighter.

Inspiration. It is the balm for the aching soul of a marriage.

For Reflection

1. Making and maintaining a genuine spiritual connection— the kind where a husband and wife share their spiritual sides in a reciprocal fashion and have a sense of union because of it—is often difficult for even the most devout couples. Why, in your opinion, is this the case?
2. Consider the following questions: On a scale of one to ten, where would you rate your desire for making a spiritual connection with your spouse? On that same scale, where would you rate the current level of the spiritual intimacy the two of you share together? What can you do to bring these numbers closer together?
3. After reading about the different spiritual temperaments or styles discussed in this chapter, where do you see yourself most often? Have you ever thought this style was the best for your partner because it worked well for you? If so, what kinds of subtle or not-so-subtle messages have you sent to your partner because of this, and what might you do to rebuild any potential damage because of them?
4. Explore the issue of inspiration. What are some of the most inspirational moments you have shared as a couple? Are they easy or difficult to remember? And what might this tell you about your need for inspiration? More important, what can you do to cultivate more inspirational moments in your marriage?

the good that comes
from a problem-solving marriage

Every day your love expands when you clearly see
you've become more richly yourselves together
than you could have ever managed alone.

*A marriage made in heaven is one where a man and
a woman become more richly themselves together than the chances
are either of them could ever have managed to become alone.*
Frederick Buechner

If there was a program that could guarantee you'd live longer, be healthier, have more happiness, save more time, and make more money starting today, would you be interested? Of course, who wouldn't? It's a stupid question—one that Madison Avenue has been bouncing off us for years. In fact, infomercials, self-help gurus, exercise machines, kitchen devices, and other gizmos have touted more promises like this than can be counted. The public pays billions of dollars each year for programs and systems that can do any one of these things. But truth be told, the real pathway to achieving all these benefits we long for is not found in a program or a device. It is found in a relationship called marriage.

If you think we are sounding overly zealous or naive, we ask you to bear with us. Throughout this entire book we have been eager to get to this last chapter, because there is so much good that comes to couples like you who aren't willing to let something bad spoil their marriage. How do we know? Because we have been on a quest for quite some time to discover the benefits of matrimony. And we have found them. These are not benefits we dreamed up and wrote down. These are benefits discovered from hard science.

So what's the good that comes from a good marriage? The answer could fill several volumes. In fact, it does, quite literally. In scientific journal articles all over this country, in every university library in the land, you will find thousands of studies that have examined the benefits of marriage from every angle. Social scientists have been busy for decades trying to quantify and measure exactly what happens to people who become husband and wife.

In this chapter we don't even begin to do justice to all the studies that have shed light on this interesting question. This is not the place for that. A scholarly literature review will be set aside in order to zero in on the fundamental facts. In this chapter, we will show you how a good marriage makes people happier, healthier, and wealthier. These are the facts no social scientist can dispute. But before we close this chapter, and this book, we leave you with one additional and final thought. It has to do with something good that comes from a good marriage—something social scientists have not yet been able to measure or quantify. And probably never will.

A Good Marriage Makes People Happy

As a college professor, I (Les) have taught Psychology 101 for more than a decade, and most of those years I have used a textbook written by one of the kindest gentlemen I've ever met. Dr. David Myers, of Hope College in Michigan, has made a special effort on more than one occasion to visit my classroom of a hundred or so students and present a guest lecture. Truth is, I invite him to my classroom more for my own benefit than for my students. Dave is arguably one of the most knowledgeable people in psychology on the planet, and I treasure the times I have been able to pick his brain. Whether it is over a cup of tea in the campus center or in my home, my mind is always expanded by his revelations. And on one occasion, knowing that most of my research and writing was on marriage, Dave told me about some work he was doing in the area of happiness. His head was filled with endless data and statistics on what makes people happy.[1] After hearing him discuss the intricacies of happiness in the human psyche, I eventually asked him a pointed question: "Can you do anything to guarantee somebody's happiness?"

He was quick with his reply: "You can't guarantee it, but the closest thing that comes to ensuring happiness in somebody's life is marriage."

Dr. Myers is not alone in his assessment. Experts in this area all agree, an emotional windfall awaits every good marriage. Even unhappily married partners benefit here, but for couples in a good marriage, the benefits are truly outstanding. Studies that follow people's lives over a number of years provide convincing evidence that marriage plainly causes better emotional health. Married men and women, for example, report fewer emotional struggles than those who are single, divorced, or widowed. That means they have less depression, less anxiety, and fewer psychological problems in general.[2] More important, people with a good marriage have more fun. Marital status is an extremely reliable predictor of happiness. One survey of fourteen thousand adults over a ten-year period found that 40 percent of married people say they are "very happy" with their life in general, compared to less than 25 percent of those who are single or who are cohabiting (only 18 percent of divorced people fall into this category).[3]

> A good wife and health,
> is a man's best wealth.
> *Benjamin Franklin*

Want another barometer of happiness for couples? How about sex? Truth is, a good marriage also means good sex. In study after study, married people have both more and better sex than singles do.[4] Contrary to the hackneyed jokes about the supposed lack of and boredom with married sex, married couples are the most sexually satisfied people on earth. Not only do married couples have sex more frequently, they enjoy it more, both physically and emotionally, than do their unmarried counterparts. Perhaps even more surprising to some, married people who attend church weekly are much more likely to be sexually satisfied than married people with less traditional values.[5] Marriage, as it turns out, does not douse the flame of passion; it is the very fan that flames our sexual fire.

A Good Marriage Makes People Healthy

A few months ago I (Les) was flying from Seattle to Washington, D.C., when the man seated across the aisle from me gasped for breath, grabbed his chest, and fell to the floor. "Is there a doctor on board?" the woman seated next to him shouted frantically. It was obvious he was having serious chest pain. Thankfully, a physician quickly emerged, and he and I carried the man toward the front of the plane. The doctor had the pilot reroute our flight to Denver, the nearest airport, where emergency personnel would be waiting. "What does he need in the meantime?" a concerned flight attendant asked. "His wife," said the doctor. She was quickly escorted to his side. She lay on the floor next to him, holding his hand and gently caressing his face. "That's the best medicine for now," the doctor whispered to me.

I don't know the end of that man's story. I hope he made it. But I do know that the kind physician I met that day knew what he was doing when he got his patient's wife by her husband's side. Research has now shown that a spouse can literally save your life. One study summed it up this way: "Compared to married people, the nonmarried … have higher rates of mortality than the married: about 50 percent higher among women and 250 percent among men."[6] Unmarried people are far more likely than married people to die from all causes—including coronary heart disease, cancer, and automobile accidents.

A good marriage not only preserves life, but it protects health as well. Married people feel physically healthier than those who are divorced, separated, or widowed, according to research.[7] Married men and women are also less likely than singles to suffer from long-term chronic illnesses or disabilities.[8]

How could a marriage certificate or a wedding band make a difference when it comes to physical health, you may be wondering. The answer is found in what social scientists call social support—and what some spouses call nagging. Married people look after each other. We make sure our partner is getting enough sleep, exercising, eating wisely, and so on. Eight out of ten married men, one study revealed, say that their wives have reminded them to do something to protect their health.[9] The point is that a good marriage makes for good health. But the good that comes from a good marriage doesn't stop there.

A Good Marriage Makes People Wealthy

"What are some of the most common myths of marriage?" We often ask this question of couples at some point during our weekend seminars. Couples huddle together for a moment or two, and then the hands start going up. And almost like clockwork, somebody will shout out: "Two can live as cheaply as one!" Of course, it is said as a joke, but in reality it is more a truth than a myth. Married people, compared to singles, are wealthier. Married men in particular make significantly more money than do bachelors. And wives are financially better off than single women, despite wives' lower personal earnings, because they share their husbands' earnings.

Can two live as cheaply as one? Not quite, but almost. After all, married people can share furnishings, a TV, a stereo, a phone line. They can spend less per person for the same lifestyle than the same individuals would if they lived separately. In other words, by virtue of being married, you are better off financially than you would be if you were single. And the longer you stay married, the more your wealth accumulates. In contrast, the length of a cohabiting couple's relationship has no effect on wealth accumulation.[10]

Why does marriage have such a profound impact on our bank accounts? Because it calls us to be more responsible. Linda Waite and Maggie Gallagher put it this way in their helpful book, *The Case for Marriage*: "When a single person is struck by the impulse to splurge rather than save, it is nobody's business but his or her own. But when a married person thinks about splurging, he or she also has to think about how to explain it to a spouse."[11] And for this very reason, the better one's marriage, the more likely it is for a couple to be more responsible with their finances. Couples in good marriages pool their money, share expenses, divide labor, keep each other from impulse spending, and thus create more opportunities for building wealth—leading some financial experts to claim that a good marriage is literally a person's most important financial asset.

So what's the good that comes from a good marriage? In a single sentence, a good marriage helps us live longer, healthier, happier, and more affluent lives. But there's another reason for battling problems when they strike your good marriage. It is a reason better than all the rest.

A Final Thought about Good Marriages

Early in this book we noted the relationship between Jack and Rose, the lead characters in the movie *Titanic*. We leave you with a final story involving the same doomed ship.

This one, however, is true, and it involves Isidor and Ida Strauss, an immigrant couple to America who scratched and scrapped their way in the new world to make a name for themselves. They built a little merchandise store in New York City and named it Macy's.

On that fateful April day in 1912, they were enjoying a much-deserved vacation and were the picture of romance as they strolled the decks of the luxury ocean liner. Late that evening as the *Titanic* was making its maiden voyage across the Atlantic, however, we all know it hit the imponderable chunk of ice below the ocean's surface.

As people scrambled for safety, Isidor and Ida Strauss walked calmly on the deck, assessing the situation before finally approaching a lifeboat in the process of being filled with women and children. As Mrs. Strauss was climbing into the lifeboat, she paused, changed her mind, turned to her husband, and said, "Where you go, I go."

Members of the crew tried to convince her that she was making a mistake. Ida wouldn't listen. A crew member turned to old Mr. Strauss and said, "I'm sure no one would object to an old gentleman like yourself getting in." But Isidor was as stubborn as his wife. "I will not go before the other men," he countered.

The issue was settled. Neither would go without the other, and neither one would go. The old couple walked to a set of nearby deck chairs, sat down together, and waited for the inevitable.

How many of us would give up our seat on the lifeboat to sit on a deck chair of the *Titanic* with the one we love? We have a hunch you would. And we'd like to think we would too. We'd do it for the immeasurable good our marriage has given us. We'd do it for each other.

In our first chapter, we made the point that all marriages start out good. And they do. They look indestructible on their wedding day, held together more strongly and tighter than the rivets holding the "unsinkable" *Titanic*. But along the way, we all hit icebergs: busyness, irritability, debt, boredom, pain, sexual unfulfillment, dishonesty, addiction, infidelity, loss, or any number of other problems. It's enough to make most mere mortals abandon ship. But we don't. You would not have read this book if that were your choice.

Because the good that comes from a good marriage is too good to discard, we each turn to our spouse and say, "I love you more than ever ... where you go, I go."

For Reflection

1. Frederick Buechner says, "A marriage made in heaven is one where a man and a woman become more richly themselves together than the chances are either of them could ever have managed to become alone." How have you become more "richly yourself" because of your marriage?

2. Research has plainly shown that marriage makes people physically healthier, emotionally healthier, and financially better off. The good that comes from a good marriage, of course, provides a unique blessing for each couple. Out of these three categories, which blessing do you most appreciate and why?

3. Some people find it extremely powerful to keep a record of things they are thankful for. Do you think that such an exercise, if applied to your marriage, would raise your level of appreciation for your marriage? No doubt. You might consider doing just that, but for right now, what are the two or three things you appreciate most about your marriage relationship?

practical help
for a marriage in crisis

*The easiest period in a crisis situation is actually the battle itself.
And the most dangerous period is the aftermath . . . [when] an
individual must watch out for dulled reactions and faulty judgment.*
Richard M. Nixon

There are cycles to this domestic life of marriage—times when you're in love and life is beautiful, and times when you coexist as amiable roommates, too busy to take much notice of each other as long as the domestic machinery is humming along. And then there are times when the gears of marriage gum up and screech to a halt. The siren is sounded and the flare gun is fired, because your marriage has hit a crisis.

For us, this happened just over three years ago. We'd conceived our first child after fourteen years of marriage. Because of complications that were not entirely clear, Leslie was ordered by her doctor to remain on round-the-clock bed rest just three months into the pregnancy. She could only leave the house for medical appointments. Six months into her pregnancy, the doctor decided to place her in the hospital. "I'm not sure what's happening," the doctor told us, "but from the sonogram we can see that your baby isn't getting the nutrition he needs. He's not growing."

With Leslie's life at serious risk, our baby boy, John, was born two weeks later through emergency C-section. He was three months premature and weighed just over a pound. He was rushed into the neonatal intensive care unit, where he was attached to monitors and machines that helped him breathe, regulate his temperature, and do everything else a tiny body needs to live.

A week later the phone woke us out of a restless sleep. It was John's primary nurse calling to tell us that our newborn son was going into emergency surgery. We raced to the hospital just in time to see his one-pound body being wheeled down the corridor of the hospital on an adult-sized gurney surrounded by two surgeons and four technicians.

Baby John's abdominal surgery was successful. For the next three months he lay in his isolette in the ICU. And every day we sat by his side in our sterile gowns as the machines around him hummed and beeped. John, weighing just over three pounds, finally came home tethered to a six-foot oxygen tank. Today, as a happy three-year-old, John has more energy than both of us combined. But those months of crisis changed our lives and our marriage forever. We know the experience of unspeakable fear together as a couple. We know what it's like to have to pull the car over because you're crying too hard. We know what it's like, as a couple, to be jolted to the core.

When "For Better or for Worse" Is Worse Than You Ever Imagined

Every marriage has a story, a plot twist, a critical moment that changes everything. Like a scarred tree after a horrific storm, the event leaves its mark in ways that will never allow us to forget its occurrence. A few words now color our entire lives:

Bill had to go to war.
We lost the money when the market crashed.

The doctor says we can't have children.
The twister ripped right through our house.

A single sentence completely alters a couple's narrative. The love story we were writing will never be the same. Unpredictable events have led us to unponderable places.

And when you survive, when you make it through these confusing head-on collisions with life, they become both the heaven and the hell of marriage. Depending, of course, on how you respond, they will make you bitter or they will make you better.

When you promised "for better or for worse," maybe you momentarily considered the possibilities of "worse": illness, problems with children, financial difficulties. But you probably never imagined that you might one day face something truly terrible, something that would shake you to the core. And now that your marriage has been jolted by this horrible thing, you feel like two punched-out prize fighters too exhausted to break the clinch, so you hang on to one another, because it's the only alternative to falling down or to throwing in the towel.

> Those things that hurt, instruct.
> *Benjamin Franklin*

This appendix is for every couple who has been jolted to the core and is still hanging on. Because of some crisis, you are not what you were, and your partner isn't either. Something you have run into has changed you and your relationship for the worse, and you're trying to make it better. While we don't know your story, we want to examine four of the most common bombshells that send spouses running for the bunker: addiction, infidelity, infertility, and loss.

We've designed this appendix so you can turn to any of the independent sections that are most relevant to you and your relationship. None of them is meant to be a magic wand for erasing your pain or repairing your marriage. But they may give you new handles for holding on to heaven while your marriage goes through hell.

Exercise 20: Taking Cover from a Bombshell and Its Fallout

If you are reading this appendix, you have probably suffered a major crisis in your marriage—something that has brought the two of you to a place you never expected. Whatever your crisis, this workbook exercise is designed to give you a preliminary platform on which to read the remainder of this chapter.

The Agony of Addiction

Six years ago, Greg Smith, a high school basketball coach, blacked out during a routine practice with his team. When he came to at the hospital that evening, a dark secret began to unravel. Greg was an alcoholic and nobody knew. For eleven years he had been secretly drinking vodka, an odorless libation he had stashed in his garage. Connie, his wife of ten years, sat in shock while Greg laid open his long-standing secret that night at the hospital.

A basketball star in college, Greg had never taken an alcoholic drink in his life until he joined some teammates one evening after a game. "The next morning when I woke up," he later told me, "all I thought about was getting another drink." He did. When he married Connie later that year, he was already well into his addiction, and she didn't have a clue.

Eleven years later, as Greg's private addiction was exposed, Connie came unglued. She called us from the hospital halfway across the country. "Did you have any idea this was happening?" We were as helpless as she was. It had to be the loneliest night of Connie's life—and her life would never be the same.

Few things divide a couple more than addiction. Whether it be with alcohol, drugs, food, or pornography, addiction is as divisive in marriage as an international border. It creates a quiet chasm that grows increasingly wider with each compulsive behavior. If your marriage has been struck by the damage of addiction, we want to make one fundamental point that may help you keep this jolt from ruining your relationship.[1]

Grief and addiction have something in common: denial. The loss of a stable marriage because of addictive involvement generates despair, anger, and loneliness. And because the loss is not as tangible as other losses (the addict is still present), losing a loved one to addiction has the potential of keeping one stuck indefinitely in the early stages of grief—and this is guaranteed to be the undoing of any relationship. Therein is the bind of the "co-addict," or the spouse who wants to mend a broken relationship and winds up unwittingly participating in the same impaired mental processes as the addict.

By definition, the addict replaces normal human relationships with compulsive behavior that is out of control. If you are married to an addict, you feel the loss, you try to deny it exists, and you become angry. In spite of your despair—or perhaps because of it—you go to extreme lengths to preserve the exterior world of your addicted spouse and your once-happy home.

That's exactly what happened to Ruth, the daughter of an alcoholic. She married James, also from an alcoholic home. In fact, part of their initial attraction was that they agreed they would never do what their parents did. Even though James drank, Ruth felt secure that he would not become an addict. That all changed, however, the night he was arrested on a drunk and disorderly charge. Ruth, embarrassed, told no one. James gave excuses for his behavior. Ruth didn't believe him but acted as if she did. Deep inside, she also believed she was partly to blame. In short, Ruth was in almost as much denial about her husband's addiction as he was. Each promise he made to abstain from alcohol made Ruth all the more certain that their problem would disappear. But it didn't.

> A habit is hell for those you love, and it's the worst kind of hell for those who love you.
> *Billie Holiday*

Eventually Ruth, with the help of a counselor, realized that she was sacrificing her own identity, giving up a part of herself in order to stay in a relationship with James. She was overlooking behavior that hurt her deeply, and she was covering up behavior she despised. She appeared cheerful when she was hurting. And most of all, she blamed herself for a problem she didn't start. Her reactions were only making her situation worse.

Ruth is a co-addict. The result? More isolation and distance from James. The reason? When there is a chance for real intimacy, it is evaded by silence or fighting. Sadly, this leads Ruth, like all co-addicts, to continue her martyrdom in an effort to make herself indispensable to her poor husband. The failure of James to provide the care and love she is longing for, however, results in further solo efforts to reform her husband. And the cycle goes on.

> With somebody to love, even the most severely afflicted can make it.
> Ken Duckworth

For some couples this sad cycle goes on for years. Not surprising, addictions of all kinds thrive in such relationships. Alcoholism and compulsive overeating may even mingle with sexual addiction in such an environment. The husband justifies his sexual addiction because "she is always drunk." The wife who gains fifty pounds as an expression of her rage is also doing something her husband can't control. Each addiction may involve different behaviors, but they are all crying out for the same remedy: responsibility. The shift of energy from blaming circumstances and other people to taking ownership for feelings and behaviors creates a new environment of trust that is the key to overcoming and recovering from any major problem.

That's what our friends Greg and Connie Smith discovered. Greg attends his AA meetings religiously, while they both continue to rebuild their relationship and celebrate his sobriety. Each of them takes responsibility, one day at a time.

The Insecurity of Infidelity

"What I am writing in this note will be shocking to you, but I can't withhold the truth any longer. I'm tired of living the lies. I'm having an affair with a man I met at work. He's younger than I, and I guess I got pulled in by his compliments and flirtations. Anyway, I can't pretend any longer. I wanted you to know the truth, and if I had more courage I'd tell you in person, but this note is the best I could do. I'm sorry. I really am. I know I've hurt you, and I never wanted to do that. I hope you will make this easy for both of us, and for our kids."

With this short note, the world falls off its axis, self-esteem is shattered, lives fall apart, and an unsuspecting spouse is left trying to pick up the pieces. Everything that was stable has been rocked by infidelity.

Research shows that about 24 percent of men and 14 percent of women have had sex outside their marriages.[2] Some argue that these numbers are far too low compared to previous studies. Anyway, the findings are hotly debated. None of that really matters, however, if infidelity has hit your home. All you care about is recovering from the powerful punch to the solar plexus of your relationship.

Is it even possible to recover? you wonder. The answer is yes. If two people are willing to slog through the pain and anger of one of the most devastating experiences a husband and wife could ever encounter, they can save their marriage.[3] There are countless couples who are living testimonies to the fact that a relationship that has been jolted by unfaithfulness can be restored. We've talked to dozens of them, and here are some of the helpful suggestions we've gleaned.

To the spouse who had the affair:

First and foremost, sever all contact with the third party immediately. Clear boundaries need to be established if you are wanting to rebuild the trust you have broken with your partner.

You must be willing to answer any questions from your spouse. This is not because your partner needs to know all the details of what went on, but they do need to know they have your willingness to give them the details. Openness to questioning shows respect, honor, and equality. It shows that you can be trusted in the future.

To the spouse who has remained faithful:

You should only ask questions if you really want the truth. Some things may be better left alone if you can do it. You must also steer clear of the temptation down the road to use any information you ask for as a way to beat up your partner for other problems.

It may take years to absorb the emotional impact of what has happened. Adultery is not something you can get over quickly. It's important to give yourself plenty of recovery time.

The number-one goal for both partners is to rebuild trust. In the weeks and months after Susan's husband, Larry, had an affair, she found herself doubting him any time he was late coming home or not available when she called him at work. For years she had never questioned him about those things, but with his infidelity fresh in her mind, she had a hard time believing his explanations. To build trust, Larry worked on changing his pattern; he tried to let Susan know if he was going out later than usual or was going to be away from the office. After a while, though, having to check in with his wife began to make him feel stifled and controlled. By then Susan could see Larry's efforts to be accountable, so she didn't need to check on

Of all the virtues we can learn, no trait is more useful, more essential for survival, and more likely to improve the quality of life than the ability to transform adversity into an enjoyable challenge.
Mihalyi Csikszentmihaly

him so much. After that, Larry's calls became an act of love rather than duty.

Catherine and Walter changed some behaviors too. Walter told Catherine the time of day when he typically felt tempted. They made a pact that he could call her for encouragement any time his mind began to wander into improper fantasies. Eventually, these calls became opportunities to express their love and passion for each other, instead of just an update on his struggle.

It's incredible to see what once appeared to be an irreparable wound transformed into a catalyst for growth in marriage. If you are struggling with betrayal of trust, know that you are already living with the "worse" in "for better or worse." With God's help and healing, even the most serious betrayal can be overcome when you make right what has gone wrong.

The Injustice of Infertility

Marcia, a thirty-two-year-old married woman: "If we can't have a baby, I'm not sure I want to be married. I've had five miscarriages in three years, and I'm just not up to dealing with my husband, Ken. He wants me to act as if nothing has happened. We've been going to an infertility clinic for three years. I wanted a child of our own more than anything in the world, and I thought Ken did too. I tried to hide my heartbreak because I could tell it made him uncomfortable, even irritable. But he has become less sympathetic with each miscarriage."

Ken, thirty-one, Marcia's husband of seven years: "I knew Marcia was upset about losing the babies, but I had no idea how unhappy she was. I'm not good at reading between the lines. I confronted her about it, but she didn't want to talk about it. She holds everything inside and lets it eat away at her. I'm not like that. If I run into a roadblock, I press on in another direction. We had no control over what happened, so I figured, you grieve, then you pick yourself up and go on. Certainly, I wanted a baby.

I was very disappointed, but a part of me was saying, 'Don't let Marcia see how much you are affected, because it will only make things worse.'"

Half of all Americans who try to get pregnant have trouble doing so, and one in six couples in the United States are jolted by infertility—the inability to conceive a child after trying for a year or more.[4] These couples not only make a financial sacrifice and commit a substantial amount of time to undergo intrusive medical tests and treatments, but their marriages are often turned inside out. What was once a passionate exchange becomes a scheduled exercise fraught with anxiety about failing again to conceive. Partners feel angry with their bodies and struggle with the thorny question of whether to keep their medical trials secret from family and friends. Hovering above all of these decisions is the disappointing possibility that there is no guarantee they will ever conceive a child.[5]

If you are struggling with the emotional assault of infertility, you know pangs of sadness like few other couples. Most likely, every area of your life is impacted—from career decisions, to sexuality, to relationships with friends and extended family members. Depending on how long you have struggled, you may have traveled through some fairly predictable passages. First, you were preoccupied with why this was happening to you. Life was put on hold while you became obsessed with questions surrounding infertility. *What have we done wrong? Why am I so defective? Why are we denied something the rest of the world takes for granted?* Next, you mourn the loss of bearing children and undergo an intense soul-searching of what parenting means to you as individuals, as a couple, and as members of your extended family and society. Finally, over time, you enter a decision-making phase about pursuing adoption or adjusting to childlessness and seeking fulfillment in other areas of life. This is also the stage in which you must realign the disjointedness your marriage has endured as a result of your journey.

A couple best does this by healing the sometimes private wounds each partner has suffered in the process. Whether you are just coming to terms with being childless as a couple or you have been at this place for many years, it is imperative for the life of your relationship that you attend to any lingering loose ends—especially the ones your partner may not know about.

In the case of Marcia and Ken, they appeared to be light-years apart in their perceptions of the problems in their marriage. Marcia was absolutely devastated by her series of miscarriages, and she desperately wanted Ken to understand the depth of her sorrow. However, rather than confront him by saying, "Look, I'm in real pain," she would cry in private. Her grief was so overwhelming she was considering turning away from Ken and their marriage altogether.

Ken's natural tendency to pick himself up and press on had been intensified by his military career. Although truly upset by the miscarriages, he coped by looking for ways to take positive action. This was interpreted by Marcia as being insensitive. Their relationship was begging for empathy and compromise.

> When is a crisis reached? When questions arise that can't be answered.
> *Ryszard Kapuscinski*

Healing came when Marcia recognized that Ken's coping mechanism was just as valid as hers. Ken was able to help her with this. "I thought I was protecting you by not expressing my own pain and disappointment," Ken told Marcia. "I do care, deeply. I realize now that the way you deal with something may be different from the way I deal with it, but that doesn't mean one of us is wrong and the other is right." These kind words were the turning point for Marcia. She was amazed by Ken's sensitivity.

Ken had concerns about their sex life too, and in a safe environment was able to talk to Marcia without being accusatory.

"For so long it has been about getting pregnant and all the romance has gone out of it for us," he said. Marcia, feeling understood and less guarded, was quick to agree.

In time, Marcia and Ken discovered an exciting and relaxing physical relationship that surpassed anything they'd had before. "It's because we are open with each other now," she explains. "For the first time, we're committed to caring for each other's wants and needs. We both want a baby, but for now we're primarily working on building our marriage. We're looking into adoption, but whatever happens we're excited about our future together."

Helping each other heal private wounds you've suffered through your own journey of infertility does not guarantee a "happy" ending of the struggle—not by a long shot—but it does significantly increase the odds of keeping infertility from tearing at the fabric of your good marriage.

Real-Life Problem Solvers

How We Found Hope in the Midst of Infertility

Mark and Victoria Eaton
Married in 1989

We'd been married eight years. Mark was at the tail end of completing his Ph.D. in Boston and I was wrapping up another year of teaching elementary school when we decided to go off birth control and have a baby. A year had passed, and we still weren't pregnant when Mark landed a job in my hometown of Oklahoma City. We thought it was all for the best. We were looking forward to Mark's first real job as a professor, and Oklahoma seemed like an ideal place to settle down and start a family.

Mark's Experience

At first I wasn't as eager to start a family as Victoria was; I thought we had plenty of time. But once we were both on board and definitely trying to get pregnant, I thought it would be easy. As the months rolled by, however, the word *infertile* began popping into my head. As the months turned into years, I began to wonder if we would ever have kids. I remained optimistic, however. Somewhat reluctantly, I went along with Victoria's desire to look into adoption, because I was clinging to the belief that it was only a matter of time before we conceived. My wife's emotional roller coaster was heartbreaking. The whole experience was extremely painful for both of us and our marriage.

Victoria's Experience

Once I realized that getting pregnant wasn't going to be easy for us, I began seeing babies everywhere I looked. At the grocery store. At church. Even sitting in traffic, I couldn't help but notice the baby seats in the back of so many cars. Of course, many of my friends had babies, and those that didn't were pregnant, or so it seemed. I tried to block it from my mind and focus on not getting stressed. Everything I read on infertility told me that stressed was the worst thing I could be as we tried to get pregnant. But it seemed everything, and everyone— including my husband—stressed me out.

How We Solved the Problem

We made a decision to work together as we walked this painful path. To balance out our obsession with having a baby, we developed healthy diversions such as athletics and adventurous travel together. I took on a new job with the Prairie Dance Theater. We also learned to steer clear of family-oriented vacation spots or malls filled with strollers at Christmas. I (Victoria) went to a psychologist who understood the pain of infertility, and we both went to a social worker for help. The most important way of dealing with the situation, probably, was to delve into the adoption process by visiting an agency in Fort Worth, Texas—the same one from which I was adopted as a baby. I also kept an extensive journal during this time and followed the book *The Artist's Way*, which helped me figure out how I could use my creativity in ways other than by creating a child. To this day, keeping a journal allows me to stand back from all difficulties and see small glimpses of light.

A Word to Other Couples

Talk with other couples who are going through problems with infertility. Sharing each other's suffering will help you survive it. And don't neglect the support of family and friends who say prayers on your behalf.

The Loneliness of Loss

On September of 1988, major league baseball player for the San Francisco Giants Dave Dravecky was diagnosed as having a tumor in his left arm—his pitching arm. Ten years to the day after marrying Jan, Dave underwent surgery to remove the tumor. The prognosis was bad. He might be lucky enough to play catch in the backyard with their son, but Dave would never pitch professionally again. But to the surprise of his doctors, Dave was eventually able to go through his pitching motion. By July of 1989 he was pitching in the minor leagues; and on August 10, 1989, Dave made a truly miraculous comeback to pitch a major league game at Candlestick Park.

A media frenzy ensued. Dave was featured on every sports page in the country. Then, just five days after the comeback game, Dave was pitching in Montreal when the bone in his pitching arm snapped; the pop could be heard around the stadium, and his career came to an abrupt end. In June 1991, Dave's arm and shoulder had to be amputated. All through this process Jan worked diligently to support her husband by talking with the media, answering mail, cooking meals, and caring for their kids. Unbeknownst to her husband, however, Jan was suffering in silence. She started having panic attacks, then developed a clinical depression that kept her from getting out of bed in the morning.

Loss, devastating loss, is like that. Few things jolt our personhood, our marriage, our very core, more severely than loss. Whether it be loss of a job through injury or circumstances, the loss of money due to a soured investment, the loss of a friend or loved one due to tragedy or natural causes, the loss of a child in a custody dispute from a previous marriage—loss creates one of the loneliest experiences on earth, even in the middle of a good marriage.

You probably know the stages: numbing disbelief, yearning and searching, disorganization and despair. Collectively we call it grief.

> Every form of addiction is bad, no matter whether the narcotic be alcohol or morphine or idealism.
> *Carl Jung*

Though highly individual, it is a process, not an event, that always takes time. It can't be rushed or compressed. The grief process, though painful in many ways, has its own internal logic; if allowed to proceed, it almost always resolves successfully. In the end, grief takes us to a new place and helps us reorganize our life and move forward.

As grief does its work, however, it can wreak havoc on a marriage, just like it did for Dave and Jan Dravecky. For this reason we want to make one simple suggestion if you are coping with loss in your life: Keep the channels of communication clear. Without an open and honest dialogue, a husband and wife will unknowingly build barriers around their hearts. They will journey separate paths and lose touch with one another. They will miss out on one of the great gifts of being married.

Keeping communication channels open requires vulnerability. It demands your real feelings. It assumes your tears will roll down each other's cheeks. Dave and Jan learned this lesson as they traveled the path of grief together. As iron sharpens iron, they helped one another through the darkest days of their marriage to create a new life that neither one of them would now trade for anything.

Keeping communication honest and open while grieving is not always safe, but it is good. In C. S. Lewis's children's book *The Lion, the Witch, and the Wardrobe*, there is a scene in which one of the main characters, a young girl named Lucy, first encounters Aslan, the great lion. Lucy sees Aslan and exclaims with trepidation to one of the talking animals, "Is he safe?" The animal responds, "Safe . . . ? Who said anything about being safe? 'Course he isn't safe. But he's good."

Grieving a loss with your spouse isn't always safe, either. It's not predictable. You can't control how each one of you will respond to frightening feelings. But the process is good. When you trust it, honest grieving—together—will keep problems from harming your marriage.

The Art of the Comeback

My father, a pastor, often says that every person will have their own private Gethsemane. It will usually happen in a familiar place. With Jesus it was in the place where he routinely prayed and where Judas knew he could find him. And our Gethsemane will probably include a Judas, someone—maybe even our spouse—who will let us down in ways we never dreamed. In our private Gethsemane we may have close friends who suddenly go to sleep when we need them the most—our Peter, James, and John. We may wonder if their telephones have been disconnected.

Exercise 21: Surviving Your Private Gethsemane

Before leaving this part of the book, we hope you will take some time to reflect on whatever has jolted your marriage and construct a positive plan for surviving it. This workbook exercise will walk you through the steps for doing just that.

However you experience your fall into the abyss, whether it is due to addiction, infidelity, infertility, or loss, you probably didn't see it coming. No amount of planning could have prevented the jolt that has struck you and your marriage. You may have had little or no control over its occurrence, but you *can* control your response to it. And that is the art of the comeback.

We know a couple, Bill and Lydia, who just about lost everything. Bill had worked for many years as an executive in a national corporation. He took early retirement, turning over his big chunk of severance pay to a friend who had a financial deal that could not miss. But it did. Bill and Lydia, both in their mid-sixties, found themselves scrambling to live on an inadequate income after their investments had drained dry. It was a huge jolt. Lesser people have been known to destroy themselves in the face of such a problem. Not Bill and Lydia. They moved from a big fashionable house to a small bungalow. They traded in their big car for a small economy model. Instead of enjoying his retirement, Bill, who could not return to his old executive position, now held a street job reading meters for a public utility company.

Bill and Lydia had every reason to be bitter. Instead, they determined to adjust their attitude to a bad thing that was beyond their control. If you met them, you would have no idea they'd ever suffered such a jolt. Though it took time to grieve their loss, they are happy, in spite of their circumstances.

We know another couple who encountered almost the same jolt as Bill and Lydia, but it was too much for them to absorb. With the loss of their retirement money, they became increasingly bitter and mean. They attended church, just like Bill and Lydia, but they rejected other people's love and concern. They became so critical that their pastor struggled to treat them with dignity. They never even tried to master the art of the comeback.

Don't allow that to happen to you and your marriage. Whatever your private Gethsemane may entail, determine to pick yourselves up, dust yourselves off, and bounce back— together. There is nothing stronger, or more fulfilling, than a marriage that has battled something bad and won.

Because loss can cover so many different areas, we've chosen to close this appendix with the stories of three couples who battled loss and overcame their own private Gethsemanes.

Real-Life Problem Solvers

How We Won over Depression

Dennis and Emily Lowe
Married in 1975

We were enjoying a good marriage when, without warning, an uninvited guest arrived. Depression. The first episode began just two years into our marriage while Emily was completing her master's in social work and Dennis was working full-time as a counselor. Our financial situation was improving and we were feeling more settled. We moved into our first house, were actively involved in our church, and were making plans for doctoral degrees when clinical depression first struck. It upended our marriage. And, unfortunately, it has paid us more than one visit during our twenty-five-year marriage.

Dennis's Experience

I didn't know what was happening to me when I first encountered depression. At the time, I was active in sports and music, had plenty of friends, enjoyed graduate work and starting a career, and was happily married. Suddenly I lost interest in almost everything. My motivation was depleted. I was exhausted, felt terribly alone, couldn't sleep, and lost my appetite. My self-esteem plummeted. My marriage was taking a dive too. I became agitated with Emily and discouraged by our relationship. Most of all, I felt guilty because I was no longer the person Emily had married. I was depressed. And, truthfully, I didn't know if she would stay. Through the years, as I have wrestled with depression, there have been times when I exclaimed, "I'm a therapist, psychology professor, Christian, and church leader—I'm not supposed to be depressed!" But still it lingers.

Emily's Experience

When Dennis became depressed, I felt I was losing the man I married. I watched him force himself to go to work and then crash when he came home. I felt terrible for him. I tried to overcompensate by taking care of tasks we used to share. But this "double duty" became too much, especially after we had children. That's when I started getting exhausted and angry. I know Dennis did not ask to be depressed, but sometimes my anger came out at him instead of the depression. Since he did not want many people to know about the depression, for years I did not ask for the support I needed. I had so many feelings bottled up inside, I thought I would burst. I wanted to be helpful and encouraging, but I was so unsure of how to help.

How We Solved the Problem

It took me (Dennis) quite a while to admit to myself and others that I was depressed. But once I did, we soon began finding ways to cope and to repair what it had done to our marriage. First of all, we got good medical care, and I was put on medication. We also entered individual and couple counseling. We both read books about depression and learned to rely more on God and our church family than we had done previously. Our times of prayer together as a couple became especially meaningful, and the support from other people at church who had experienced depression began to fill our lives. As we talked with other couples who had or were going through the same thing, we felt our spirits buoyed. In time, we reaffirmed our dedication to each other and gave ourselves time away from our usually hectic lives to heal. Today, we don't expect depression to never return, but when it does, we are ready to take it on—together.

A Word to Other Couples

If depression strikes your marriage, seek professional help. If you work together as a couple with a competent counselor, you can overcome it. There is hope for serious depression.

Real-Life Problem Solvers

HOW WE FOUND JOY
WITH A DISABLED CHILD

Norm and Joyce Wright
Married in 1959

We had just bought our second home and were expecting our second child—all in the same year. Our eight-year marriage was brimming with excitement and eager anticipation. I (Norm) was working as a youth pastor at a local church and teaching a couple courses at a seminary near our new home in Southern California. I (Joyce) was settling into life as mom, and life could not have been much sweeter. The day Matthew was born we were thrilled beyond words. But in his eighth month of life, he suffered the first of many grand mal seizures and was diagnosed as "profoundly mentally retarded with brain damage." He would live his entire life with the intelligence and function of an eighteen-month-old baby.

Norm's Experience

When I learned Matthew had mental impairments, I can hardly put into words my reaction. To say I was shocked would be an understatement. I was simply bowled over. It never entered my mind that we would have a child so severely impaired. In my counseling I had worked with children who were disabled, but my own son? It took me months to uncork my feelings about this. Like most men, I did quite a job of keeping them bottled up for a while. But once I came to terms with this, the feelings flowed. I grieved that my son would never be normal. I grieved and then grieved some more.

Joyce's Experience

No matter what his condition, I wanted Matthew to be loved and cared for. Of course I felt the pain and loss at the depths of my being, but I had overwhelming compassion for this boy of ours and wanted to be sure he got the best care. This desire eventually led me to the point of physical exhaustion. After all, it was like having a sixty-pound infant that was eight or nine years old. He could not be toilet trained; he could not feed himself. Everything had to be done for him, and my mothering instinct went into overdrive until I found some balance.

How We Coped with the Problem

The first step toward coping came when we were honest about our feelings. We had to admit the loss of some of our most important dreams. I (Norm) was a father of a son, but at the same time, I did not know what it was like to be the father of a son. Same was true for Joyce as a mom. We had to be honest with how low our hearts had sunk, and we had to do it in specific terms. We had to admit our lives would never be the same. This is what permitted the grieving. Our family name would not be perpetuated. We would miss all the fun of normal developmental passages with this child. These confessions helped us move forward.

The second step for us came when we began to increase our knowledge—not only of Mathew's condition but of how he would impact our marriage. More than 80 percent of couples with disabled children end up divorcing. We weren't about to let that happen to us.

Next, we found healing in talking with others about our experience. Though it was sometimes tough to get to church, we always made it a priority and enjoyed a supportive community. In time, we talked with other couples who had disabled children, and I (Norm) began to lecture and speak on it.

It was also therapeutic for us to find moments of joy in spite of our difficulties. To hear Matthew laugh was a highlight of our week. To see his older sister treat him with compassion lifted our hearts. On a more practical note, we worked diligently to create time for our marriage. As a couple we needed escapes. So once we had a trusted caretaker, we scheduled getaways that we treasure to this day.

Matthew died in 1990, but he lives on in our hearts, and the lessons we learned from him will never be forgotten.

A Word to Other Couples

Be honest with each other about specific disappointments, and find beams of joy in the midst of your pain.

Real-Life Problem Solvers

HOW WE DEALT
WITH A REBELLIOUS CHILD

Dave and Jan Stoop
Married in 1957

We never expected to have a son with a drug problem. And we never knew what a problem like this could do to a marriage. We had been married sixteen years and I (Dave) was working on a church staff as associate pastor when one of our sons got involved with the wrong crowd. At thirteen, he was well on his way to becoming a full-blown drug addict. This was the beginning of a fifteen-year journey of pain that we thought would never end. For ten years he was a heroin addict, and much of that time we had no idea where he was, or whether he was even alive.

There was very little in the way of help for the problem at that time, and none of our friends understood—*we* didn't even understand. For us, it seemed like there was no one we could talk to about what we were experiencing.

Dave's Experience

I was in complete denial. For at least the first three years of my son's problem, I thought we just had a behavioral issue that he would outgrow. It would take several more years before I fully realized the seriousness of what we faced. And for this very reason, I became my son's chief "enabler." I, more than anyone, was clueless. Jan knew the problem was more serious, but I wouldn't listen. I minimized my son's problems and thereby made them worse.

Jan's Experience

I was in a form of denial most of the early years as well, but somehow I knew that we were in trouble with this son. I couldn't get Dave to see the problem as I saw it. So when I tried to be strong and tough, Dave would undermine me and protect our son. Of course, that aggravated me all the more and pushed the two of us farther apart at times. For me, it was as if a bomb had gone off in our home and I was the only one seeing the damage. However, there were times when our roles were reversed temporarily, and Dave would see trouble that I didn't see. As a couple, we just couldn't get on the same page at the same time.

How We Coped with the Problem

After trying more than ten different recovery programs for our son, we came upon one that required our whole family to be in treatment as well. By this time we knew the scope of the problem, but we didn't know what to do differently. This treatment program finally got us on the same page with each other in dealing with the problem, so that as a couple we presented a united front to our son.

The other thing that kept us together as a couple throughout those painful years was a habit we started earlier in our marriage—we had started praying together every day, and continued to do that throughout those fifteen years, and still do today. Even when we were at odds with each other in what we were doing or saying to our son, when it came time to pray together, God would bring our spirits together.

Our son has been in recovery now for many years. As we look back, there were many points at which we could have given up on him and each other. Thank God, we didn't. Today, we are grateful for the lessons we've learned. More than anything, we know that God is faithful.

A Word to Other Couples

There's something powerful about a husband and wife meeting together in prayer for a son or a daughter. It will carry you safely through whatever dark times befall your marriage.

For Reflection

1. Do you know another couple who has been jolted by something beyond their control? How did they handle it, and what can you learn from their ways of coping?
2. Has your marriage hit a plot twist? What critical moment changed everything for the two of you, and are you happy with your response to it? If not, what might you have done differently to cope more effectively?
3. What words would you use to describe your major marriage jolt? Has it given you the capacity to respond with more compassion to others in your life that are going through their own private Gethsemane? How so?
4. On a scale of one to ten, how would you rate your comeback? What are you doing, even this week, to help steady the foundation of your marriage since this jolt has hit?

When written in Chinese the word *crisis*
is composed of two characters.
One represents danger,
and the other represents opportunity.
John F. Kennedy

notes

Chapter 1: Love Is Not Enough

1. Sheldon Vanauken, *A Severe Mercy* (New York: Harper and Row, 1977). We first described the impact this book had on our relationship in our book *Saving Your Marriage Before It Starts* (Grand Rapids: Zondervan, 1995).

2. K. Kayser, "The Process of Marital Disaffection," *Family Relations* 39 (1990): 257–65.

3. Mike Mason, *The Mystery of Marriage* (Portland, OR: Multnomah Press, 1985).

Chapter 2: Why Every Marriage Has Everyday Problems

1. J. M. Gottman and J. Gottman, "The Marriage Survival Kit: A Research-Based Marital Therapy," in *Preventative Approaches in Couples Therapy,* ed. Rony Berger and Mo Therese Hannah (Philadelphia, PA: Brunner/Mazel, 1999).

Chapter 3: Tackle This Problem First . . .
and All Others Get Easier

1. Chuck Swindoll, *Improving Your Serve* (Waco, TX: Word, 1981).

2. Viktor Frankl, *Man's Search for Meaning* (New York: Simon and Schuster, 1984).

3. Nell Mohoney, "Beliefs Can Influence Attitudes," *Kinsport Times News* (July 25, 1986): 4B.

4. Alan Loy McGinnis, *The Balanced Life* (Minneapolis: Augsburg, 1997), 53.

Chapter 4: Who Said Sex Was a Problem?

1. Kahlil Gibran, *The Prophet* (New York: Knopf, 1995), 15–16.
2. John Gottman and N. Silver, *The Seven Principles for Making Marriage Work* (New York: Crown, 1999).
3. Ibid.
4. Patricia Love and Jo Robinson, *Hot Monogamy* (New York: Plume, 1999).
5. D. W. Winnicott, *Maturational Processes and the Facilitating Environment* (New York: International Universities Press, 1965).

Chapter 5: The Six Subtle Saboteurs of Every Marriage

1. Wayne M. Sotile and Mary O. Sotile, "Working Fewer Hours Doesn't Ensure a Happy Marriage," *USA Today* (February 1, 1999).
2. Quoted in Dean Ornish, *Love and Survival* (New York: HarperCollins, 1998), 96.
3. Alain Sanders, "Job vs. Family," *Time* (December 13, 1999): 63.
4. Ron and Judy Blue, *Money Talks and So Can We* (Grand Rapids: Zondervan, 1999), 68.
5. C. Crosby, "Financial Gain, Less Pain," *Marriage Partnership* (Winter 1999): 51.
6. G. P. Parker, E. A. Barrett, and I. B. Hickie, "From Nurture to Network: Examining Links Between Perceptions of Parenting Received in Childhood and Social Bonds in Adulthood," *American Journal of Psychiatry* 149 (1992): 877–85.

Chapter 6: How to Solve Any Problem in Five (Not-So-Easy) Steps

1. Our understanding of hope and its ingredients has been shaped in large part by the writings and lectures of Lewis Smedes at Fuller Theological Seminary.
2. Lewis Smedes, *Standing on the Promises* (Nashville: Nelson, 1998), 7.
3. Karl Menninger, "Hope," in *The Nature of Man,* ed. Simon Donier (New York: Harper and Row, 1962), 186.
4. Beth Azar, "Defining the Trait that Makes Us Human," *APA Monitor* 28 (1997): 1.
5. Doug Kingsriter, "A Husband's Confession," *Christian Herald* (May/June 1991): 52.
6. Lewis Smedes, *The Art of Forgiveness* (Nashville: Moorings, 1996).
7. Gordon McDonald, "How to Experience Forgiveness from the Heart," *Christian Herald* (May/June 1991): 19.

8. When forgiving a moral wrong in a marriage, most of us need to remember that forgiveness is like grief. You can be healed of pain and anger, but a memory might make the scar break open. The important thing is not to have forgiven, but to be in the process of forgiving.

9. Scott Stanley, *The Heart of Commitment* (Nashville: Nelson, 1998).

Chapter 7: Joining Your Spirits Like Never Before

1. Gary Thomas, *Sacred Pathways* (Grand Rapids: Zondervan, 2000).

2. It's no coincidence that we so often feel inspired by our friends Neil and Marylyn. They wrote the book on it. Literally. The same day they gave Baby John his tricycle, Neil gave us a copy of his wonderful book *Catching the Rhythm of Love* (Nashville: Nelson, 2000), where he writes so eloquently of this quality and many others.

Conclusion: The Good That Comes from a Problem-Solving Marriage

1. David G. Myers, *The Pursuit of Happiness: Discovering the Pathway to Fulfillment, Well-Being, and Enduring Personal Joy* (New York: Avon, 1993).

2. John Mirosky and Catherine E. Ross, *Social Causes of Psychological Distress* (New York: Aldine De Gruyter, 1989).

3. James A. Davis, "New Money and Old Man/Lady, and 'Two's Company': Subjective Welfare in the NORC General Social Surveys, 1972–1982," *Social Indicators Research* 15 (1984): 319–50.

4. Scott Stanley and Howard Markman, *Marriage in the Nineties* (Denver: Prep Inc., 1997).

5. William R. Mattox, Jr., "What's Marriage Got to Do with It: Good Sex Comes to Those Who Wait," *Family Policy* (February 1994): 1–7.

6. Catherine E. Ross, John Mirowsky, and Karen Goldsteen, "The Impact of the Family on Health: Decade in Review," *Journal of Marriage and the Family* 52 (1990): 1061.

7. Beth A. Hahn, "Marital Status and Women's Health: The Effect of Economic Marital Acquisitions," *Journal of Marriage and the Family* 55 (1993): 495–504.

8. Mike Murphy, Karen Glaser, and Emily Grundy, "Marital Status and Long-term Illness in Great Britain," *Journal of Marriage and the Family* 59 (1997): 156–64.

9. Ebra Umberson, "Family Status and Health Behaviors: Social Control as a Dimension of Social Integration," *Journal of Health and Social Behavior* 28 (1987): 306–19.

10. Ronald R. Rindfuss and Audre VandenHeuvel, "Cohabitation: Precursor to Marriage or Alternative to Being Single?" *Population and Development Review* 16 (1990): 703–26.

11. Linda J. Waite and Maggie Gallagher, *The Case for Marriage* (New York: Doubleday, 2000), 116.

Appendix: Practical Help for a Marriage in Crisis

1. It must be clear that anyone who is suffering from addiction needs treatment. Addiction is a serious problem that requires professional intervention. If you or your spouse is struggling with alcohol or drug abuse or dependence of any kind, you must know that this is not a problem that will gradually go away on its own. Addicts need professional help. And if they have been unsuccessful in outpatient treatment programs, they probably need intensive treatment by professionally trained staff in a hospital setting. In addition, many recovering addicts find tremendous support in staying with their sobriety through psychoeducational programs, the largest and most widely known of which is Alcoholics Anonymous, with more than a million members. Their Twelve Steps and "one-day-at-a-time" philosophy have been successfully applied to numerous addictions, and they can be located in your local phone directory.

2. K. S. Peterson, "Affairs," *USA Today* (December 21, 1998).

3. Frank Pittman, *Private Lies* (New York: Norton, 1989), 121–25.

4. Beth Cooper-Hilbert, "The Infertility Crises," *Networker* (November/December 1999): 65–76.

5. Eventually, about 50 percent of those couples will conceive and bear a child, while the remaining couples grapple with the dilemma of adoption.

Bring the Parrotts to your community!

Visit *www.RealRelationships.com*

Drs. Les and Leslie Parrott are internationally known, bestselling authors. They have been featured on *Oprah*, CBS *This Morning*, CNN, *The View*, and in *USA Today* and the *New York Times*. They are also frequent guest speakers and have written for a variety of magazines. The Parrotts are hosts of the national radio broadcast *Love Talk*.

They are codirectors of the Center for Relationship Development at Seattle Pacific University, a groundbreaking program dedicated to teaching the basics of a good relationship. Les Parrott is a professor of clinical psychology and Leslie is a marriage and family therapist, both at SPU.

The Parrotts are authors of the award-winning *Saving Your Marriage Before It Starts*, *Becoming Soul Mates*, *Mentoring Engaged and Newlywed Couples* (video curriculum), *Questions Couples Ask*, and *Getting Ready for the Wedding*. Les and Leslie are currently serving as governor's marriage ambassadors for the Oklahoma ten-year Marriage Initiative.

resources by Les and Leslie Parrott

Books
Becoming Soul Mates
Getting Ready for the Wedding
I Love You More
I Love You More Workbooks
Love Is
The Love List
Love Talk
Love Talk Workbooks
The Marriage Mentor Manual
Meditations on Proverbs for Couples
Questions Couples Ask
Relationships
Relationships Workbook
Saving Your Marriage Before It Starts
Saving Your Marriage Before It Starts Workbooks
Saving Your Second Marriage Before It Starts
Saving Your Second Marriage Before It Starts Workbooks

Video Curriculum—Zondervan*Groupware*™
I Love You More
Love Talk
Mentoring Engaged and Newlywed Couples
Relationships
Saving Your Marriage Before It Starts

Audio Pages®
Love Talk
Relationships
Saving Your Marriage Before It Starts
Saving Your Second Marriage Before It Starts

Books by Les Parrott III
The Control Freak
Helping Your Struggling Teenager
High Maintenance Relationships
The Life You Want Your Kids to Live
Seven Secrets of a Healthy Dating Relationship
Shoulda, Coulda, Woulda
Once Upon a Family

Books by Leslie Parrott
If You Ever Needed Friends, It's Now
God Loves You Nose to Toes
Marshmallow Clouds

Saving Your Marriage Before It Starts
Seven Questions to Ask
Before (and After) You Marry
Drs. Les & Leslie Parrott

Do you long for real, honest advice from a couple who knows the hopes and struggles of today's couples? Do you want to build a marriage that will last a lifetime? *Saving Your Marriage Before It Starts* shows engaged couples and newlyweds how they can identify and overcome stumbling blocks to a healthy marriage.

Hardcover: 0-310-49240-8

*Workbooks Available

The Love List
Eight Little Things That Make
a Big Difference in Your Marriage
Drs. Les & Leslie Parrott

This little book will make a big impact on your marriage. Start right away applying its hands-on concepts. You'll immediately increase intimacy, gain new direction, enjoy more laughter, and much more.

Hardcover: 0-310-24850-7

Relationships
An Open and Honest Guide
to Making Bad Relationships Better
and Good Relationships Great
Drs. Les & Leslie Parrott

Today more than ever, people long for connection. In an age marked by isolation and loneliness, they measure riches in terms of belonging, acceptance, vulnerability, honesty, closeness, and commitment. And what they most want to know is how to make bad relationships better and good relationships great. Drs. Les and Leslie Parrott understand firsthand our deep need for relationships; and as relationship experts, they know what it takes to build strong, lasting bonds.

Hardcover: 0-310-20755-X   Softcover: 0-310-24266-5

*Workbooks Available

Love Talk
Speak Each Other's Language
Like You Never Have Before
Drs. Les and Leslie Parrott

Couples consistently name "improved communication" as the greatest need in their relationships. *Love Talk* is a deep yet simple plan full of new insights that will revolutionize communication in love relationships. Includes The Love Talk Indicator, a free personalized online assessment ($30.00 value).

Hardcover: 0-310-24596-6
Softcover: 0-310-26343-3

Audio: 0-310-26214-3

Just the Two of Us
Love Talk Meditations for Couples
Drs. Les & Leslie Parrott

Les and Leslie Parrott share communication insights and wisdom for couples that are newly married or have been married for forty years. The Parrotts write in a very compelling and transparent way using their personal experiences with communication challenges in their own marriage. A wonderful companion to Love Talk. Some of the titles of the meditations include: What Were You Thinking?, You're Reading My Mind, and The Talks That Tie Us Together.

Gift book: 0-310-80381-0

Love Talk Starters
275 Questions to Get
Your Conversations Going
Drs. Les & Leslie Parrott

In this companion book, *Love Talk Starters*, you will find engaging, intriguing, and revealing conversation starters. Some questions are just for fun, some will educate you about your spouse's life, and still others will drill down on some more serious topics. Use these simple conversation starters and begin communicating your way into a happier, healthier, and stronger relationship today.

Softcover: 0-310-81047-7